Sleep, Creep, Leap

The First Three Years of a Nebraska Garden

Benjamin Vogt

BOOKS BY BENJAMIN VOGT

Afterimage: Poems (SFA Press)

Without Such Absence (Finishing Line Press)

Indelible Marks (Pudding House)

http://monarchgard.com

Contents

2007-2008

3   First Garden First
5   Much Mulch
7   A Rock. A Stone. A Mountain.
9   Fore!
12 The Circuit
16 Cassia Hebecarpa – Wild Senna
17 Skin
20 The Perfect Hole
22 So Much Depends Upon a Woodchip…
26 The Research Assistant Couldn't Experiment
    With Plants Because He Hadn't Botany
28 Hatchback Trees

2009

33 650 Crocus Bulbs
34 Fire Pit / Bird Bath
36 Geum Triflorum – Prairie Smoke
37 Mr. Mows All the Time
40 UPS. FedEx. USPS.
42 The Naming
45 Deadheading Grasshoppers
48 The King is Dead. Long Live the King.
49 Parthenium Integrifolium – Wild Quinine
50 Ambergate Gardens
51 New Model Year
53 Dragonfly
55 Liatris Ligulistylis – Meadow Blazing Star
56 I Succumb to You Autumn, Like a Memory

2010

61 Rapture
62 The Geese, The 50, The Iris, The Waiting

63   Pulsatilla Vulgaris – Pasque Flower
64   Fetch
66   Dogfighting
69   Danaus Plexippus
72   Favorites
74   Tall Plants
80   Splendor in the Grass
82   The Lesser of Two Weevils
84   Thrashing
85   Confessions
87   Salvia Azurea 'Nekan' – Pitcher Sage
88   Where I'm From
90   Open Garden
92   Garden Spider
94   Aster Laevis – Smooth Aster
95   The Last Cosmo
96   Twilight Geese in Autumn

Appendix

99   Native Plant & Prairie Ecosystem Resources

Images

2   Garden in 2008
11   Pulsatilla vulgaris
19   Dodecatheon meadia
25   Clematis virginiana
32   Garden in 2009
35   Colaptes auratus
44   Echinacea purpurea
54   Dragonfly on Liatris
60   Garden in 2010
68   Monarch on Asclepias incarnata
79   Rudbeckia maxima
91   Main Back Garden in July
98   Garden Entrance in 2011

Compared to gardeners, I think it is generally agreed that others understand very little about anything of consequence.

— Henry Mitchell

2007-2008

The wonder of gardening is that one becomes a gardener by becoming a gardener. Horticulture is sometimes described as a science, sometimes as an art, but the truth is that it is neither, although it partakes of both endeavors. It is more like falling in love, something which escapes all logic. There is a moment before one becomes a gardener, and a moment after—with a whole lifetime to keep on becoming a gardener.

— Allen Lacy

Garden in 2008

First Garden First

To be fair, this isn't my first garden. Technically. And if I really get anal about it, perhaps my first garden was a green bean plant in a Styrofoam cup growing on the window ledge of my first grade classroom. I still remember the smell of that particular soil— very sweet, like sugary cigar smoke mixed with rose petals. Something like that. I remember sticking my finger in the dirt, probing for the bean seed underneath, the feathery give of that soil, the wonder—had the seed opened yet? Was it coming toward the surface? Then the two leaves. Then four. Every morning I'd check on the progress, along with my classmates, and during the day I'd glance over from my desk at the small cup with my name scribbled across the front, uncomfortably angled down the curve so it looked like a crazy person wrote it.

But if one is talking about several plants in the ground, my first garden was out the front patio of my townhome when I moved to Lincoln in 2003 to begin my PhD. The covenants said I could plant things, and that was all my green thumb mother needed to hear. "You need something out here, to give it some life, some character," she said standing out front after helping me move boxes in with my dad. "You'll be much happier for it," she continued, her arms folded across her chest, surveying the grass and vinyl siding, then looking back over her shoulder. "Trust me. Let's find a nursery."

So we borrowed my dad's SUV, picked up lavender, coneflowers, coreopsis, penstemon, a butterfly bush, a rose of sharon on a stick, some arborvitae and boxwood, some plastic edging. When we came back with a full truck my dad asked if we bought the whole store. It seemed like it to me.

Though I was looking forward to the plants, to a mini garden of about thirty square feet, I didn't really understand what it meant—not to me, or my mother, who I grew up gardening with. Her garden was split in two: maybe two thousand or more square feet out back, and at least that much out front. I often went to nurseries with her early in the morning each summer, sometimes just to get out of the noisy house. I didn't know hardly anything about growing plants.

My little patio garden in Nebraska was hard work. Thick, wet clay from a sprinkler system that overwatered and made the spade weigh an extra ten pounds. A full day of ripping up grass and planting on the south side in August made me question another proposed trip to the nursery. I had two dozen plants in the ground, raised a few inches in the clay, mulched, watered in. Plants. What now? My parents left me on my own a day later.

Over the years I taught myself how to deadhead by trial and error, never once consulting the internet, and maybe just a few times my mother. "How's the garden going?" She'd ask on the phone, and I'd reply sheepishly, humbled by the thought that this small space might be called the "G" word. "Going good. Everything doubled in size this year. I even saw a big yellow butterfly on the butterfly bush today." My mom's voice jumped as she said, "Oh, I bet that's a swallowtail. Aren't they neat?" And I supposed they were. Slowly, ever so slowly, I was getting into my manageable space. An hors d'oeuvre, in many respects. Something that I never consciously connected to my childhood or my mother, and never, until I proposed to my girlfriend and we started house hunting, something I thought of taking much further.

The last summer in the townhome I carved out another ten square feet along the sidewalk and put in some liatris, snow-in-summer, a few more coneflowers, an aster. I didn't really know what I was doing, but ripping up the sod I knew I'd caught a bug. Those ten feet were a watershed moment, a dam cracking and soon to break. As I babied the new plants with topsoil and mulch, and kneeled on the hard cement pushing my finger into the sweet earth—exploring their growing root zones and pulling out the smallest weeds—I emerged from nearly thirty years of a blurred life I didn't recognize into a world that suddenly seemed more like home, something I'd always been a part of but never really knew.

Much Mulch

It's late morning already, and we've finally made it to the new house. In two weeks we'll move in, married on 7/7/7, but until then—and before the sod gets laid—my fiancée and I are here to spread mulch. Twenty yards.

The sun feels as if it's being reflected off of a series of mirrors, each mirror focusing the heat and light. The air is thick and it's windy, carrying the musky smell of a nearby farm. I slide a wheelbarrow out of my hatchback and give my wife two buckets— she insists that buckets will be easier.

On the east side of the house, on an empty lot, is a dump truck load of wood mulch. Three quarters of it will go behind the house, the rest out front. We dig in. I map out the edges of the garden by outlining it with wheelbarrow loads, and my wife fills in the soil one small bucket at a time. "Are you sure you don't want to go buy another wheelbarrow?" I ask, and she insists that it'd just be too cumbersome and heavy. And she may be right.

After a few loads I see how long this will take. My wife has already retreated twice into the house to rinse out mulch dust from her contact lenses, and I'm beginning to feel like a slave driver. We must establish a rhythm ingrained in me during my childhood: years of spreading hay in dirt basements each winter for my dad as he built houses, untold rooms swept as workers installed plumbing and electrical, and hours of mowing weeds on empty lots—all of these $5 per hour jobs ensured me that steady repetition was key to surviving. One must retreat deep inside one's head and make a whole comatose world out of manual labor, and to get there meant emotionless efficiency. My wife disagreed, as I stopped to encourage her with a hug as she cried out the grime and heat.

Each load I jammed in more mulch into the corners of the wheelbarrow, tempting fate and gravity. As we finished about 200 square feet we approached the soggy part of the future garden, and I laid down a mulch bridge that quickly absorbed the water. Several times I got stuck and my wife pulled the wheelbarrow as I pushed, once with the load spilling out to the side like a S'Dumpr truck. Yet I kept adding mulch, even half shovel fulls, then finally individual pieces—anywhere I could in each load. When I went home and found mulch in my socks, pockets, and underwear, I saved them in a container to bring back.

Soon my skin color changed, from red to brown as the mulch dust glued to my sweat, perhaps having the side benefit of working as sunscreen. "You want to go inside, take a drink, cool off?" I'd ask my wife. "We could just go home," she'd reply, but then refill her 10 gallon bucket and carry on.

It hit me what the neighbors might think, what they'd guess or assume about us or our project. No one has any landscaping within a solid one block radius, just grass up to the foundation walls of each house. And no trees. Not even street trees planted by the developer or city. Instead of lawn, one might assume, we'd have a field of mulch, an expanse of violently shredded trees that after a rain shower left the yard smelling like sweet leather or tannin. Or like the woods I grew up around in Minnesota. Indeed, perhaps subconsciously, the olfactory sense of smell—the oldest sense in the human body—was now enacting itself from deep within. I was creating not just a home with my soon to be wife, but I was creating the home. One mulch chip at a time.

A Rock. A Stone. A Mountain.

Before we moved in, I dragged my wife over to the new house and we'd sit on the back patio steps getting a feel for the landscape. One evening it was after a rain storm, and the grade allowed for a stream to develop running from a new pond on the lot next door, across our lot at a slight diagonal, and to the lot on the other side. A dry stream, I noted. An arroyo. I couldn't plant sedum there.

Though I had a list of dozens of plants I wanted, for the wetter area I could only think of irises. Japanese irises. Whatever the nursery had. They also had a Louisiana iris called black gamecock, a dark, nearly black purple with yellow median strips running down the petal throats. Everyone sold these. A year or two later I discovered more Louisiana irises, and copper iris, but that's besides the point. I'd eventually overdose on irises until I started giving them away to my compost pile—I never saw an insect visit a single bloom.

The first summer all we had in the garden were some stark looking coneflowers, a few miscanthus, and a burgeoning collection of iris fanning into the air from an occasionally soppy bed of fresh mulch. I was lining this undercurrent with iris, creating a river of iris. I scooped up 10 pound shovel fulls of moist clay mixed with sand, wood shards, sawdust, nails, and clipped wiring left over from home construction (do those things make good soil amendments?).

It wasn't too long until the tip of my spade clanged into a chuck of what I thought was concrete. I excavated left and right, every direction, widening the circle to a two then three foot diameter. I got on my knees and poked away clumps of dirt. A rock! I felt like the archaeologist I thought I'd be when I was twelve playing with "mummified" G.I. Joes in a sandbox.

After an hour I pried the rock out of the ground, it constantly having been sucked back in like a shoe in a pile of mud. Pink, 18" on the long side, a foot wide, a foot tall, it was perfect. It was beautiful. It was mine. I could place it in the middle of the garden and in all the flatness it'd seem as if glaciers left it there, all by itself, eons ago, to watch over the memory of mammoth bones farmers still find in their Nebraska fields.

It must be granite. It was cool to the touch, and that relief rushed up my tanned arms to my sweltering face and grounded me. The surface was smooth yet gently ridged, one side tapered and wedge-shaped, the other wider and with a sort of step worn into it, until the sides slid down a pleasing angle. At around thirty pounds this rock, this stone, this mountain was a symbol of my work in the garden, of all I hoped to achieve.

In the early evening I moved my stone to where the garden path forked apart, and saw it as a compass or a sundial, something that gave evidence to the forces at work here. For what seemed the first time I was discovering what it meant to spend eight hours a day in a place without knowing I had.

Four!

We've just come back from picking up sandwiches from our favorite local shop. There's nothing I enjoy more than eating dinner on the covered deck in summer, looking out over the garden and birdfeeders. My wife and I sit in silence, voracious for Philly steak and cheese, fingers covered in wonderful grease, the foil wrap scraping our fingers as we reach for sour cream and onion chips.

Surveying all that we own—a "massive" .2 acres—we hear blue jays squawking and brown thrashers chasing each other through cedars. From right to left squirrels fly across the balance beam of the chain link fence, placed along the back property line so we could see through to our neighbor's three acre field and pretend it was our own.

The empty lot next door has a small hill in the back that rises about 10 feet to the sloping edge of our neighbor's acreage. Late one night I heard men's voices and trucks beeping, then mechanical sounds like dozens of bodies being secretly dumped into a hole. The next morning three new oak trees were scattered near the property line. Who plants trees late at night?

During dinner I lift my head from the onions and peppers and melted swiss cheese to see our neighbor appear suddenly on the top of the hill taking chip shots at golf balls. He's launching nearly invisible balls toward his house 80 yards away.

He looks over his shoulder at us. I can't believe we make eye contact, but we do, and it feels like an eternity. He slowly looks down to his ball, lines up the club, and takes a good long, arcing swing.

Then he looks at us again, bends down, places another ball. I'm not even eating any more. I nudge my wife.

This swing doesn't seem as graceful as the last—it is wide and sloppy, hasty. Is he trying to perform?

He turns his body a little toward us. Hello, I say to myself out loud, my wife laughs and says "Be quiet!" Then she says just as loudly, "What the heck is he doing?"

"Maybe he's checking us out. Sizing us up." My wife shrugs and takes a bite of her sandwich. The man chips at a ball, then leans on his club, looking out over his small field of goldenrod and immature wild cedars. A kid could get lost in that acreage playing hide-and-go-seek.

"Did you hear those trucks the other night?" I ask my wife.

"What? No," she replies.

"They planted some oaks out back."

"At night?" she says, while out of the corner of her eye watching the man watching his landscape.

"Yeah. Kinda creapy."

"He looks creepy," she says. "With that moustache and all. Why does he keep looking over here?"

After a few minutes our neighbor tosses his golf club over his shoulder nonchalantly like a civil war rifle and waddles off toward his house. We lose sight of him behind the taller cedars along our fence and finish eating so I can go dig in a few more plants before sunset.

For years I find golf balls against our property line, some half buried in mud, perhaps rising from the depths through frost heaves and rain. One day, I'm sure, I'll find one in a planting hole. A message, perhaps, like a horse head.

Pulsatilla vulgaris – Pasque Flower

The Circuit

Rows and rows of plants lay on tables waist high, their leaves still speckled with the morning watering. The air is rich, sweet, musky, a breeze nudges you and the bees toward blooms several rows over—something you hadn't noticed at first in the cacophony of flesh. For a moment it's almost as if you can see those ultraviolet runway lights that guide in pollinators, you too are part of the process. You woke this morning for a singular purpose, and this exhaustion is a subtle joy.

Once or twice each week in 2008, the first full year of the garden, I ventured to nurseries. It was often the first thing I did in the morning, and I had an itinerary, an agenda, and two shopping lists—"need" and "surprise me, baby, oh please surprise me."

10am Nursery #1

I hit the closest nursery, about ten minutes from home and in the middle of the city. From my previous twenty trips over the spring I know that here I'm likely to find the staples: salvia, coneflowers, coreopsis, monarda, and a good collection of groundcovers. Shrubs are also the cheapest here.

There's an awning over the front doors, both which swing in to a large knickknack showroom with a low ceiling. A single air conditioning duct runs the length of the room above the two cash registers. The clerks at the front greet me, but in my mission I smile and wave them off, making a quick zip line approach to the back door and out past the covered area of annuals—each one advertising itself like a woman behind plexiglass in the Amsterdam red light district. I don't need to waste money on a cheap, one time thrill, so I'm out the next door, to the tables laying in sunshine and a small lot of shrubs and trees.

I think I'm here for just a few things, so I quickly grab a one gallon plant that's on my list, then another, pinching them between my fingers and dangling them against my right side. Just for kicks I peruse a few more lanes, perhaps noticing that the threadleaf coreopsis speaks to me today in a siren song I hadn't anticipated, and I figure I know a place it will work well, to fill in a void that may only be metaphysical in my life.

Two more gallon pots and I'm pinching four of them, two in each hand. I feel like a lobster. Before I know it I'm hovering over a stand of groundcover sedum, and already picking them up in my mind. If I only had telekinesis. I can see them in my hands, in my car, in the garden. I'm lost. Hopelessly lost. And this is how it often happens. In the first year of planting—when I spend 6-8 hours outside in almost any weather save tornados—I am completely insane, full of blood lust, chlorophyll lust.

I soon have a cart full of plants, a dozen or more, and the young woman at the front asks me, as she pulls each plant from my cart and sets them into cardboard flats, if I found everything ok. I smirk, and swear she can see the saliva dripping from the corner of my mouth before I wipe it away.

11am Nursery #2

Another ten minutes east and in the north part of town is perhaps my favorite nursery. They're the smallest one I frequent, and something about them oozes class, or some sense of horticultural sophistication. I've never been able to quite put my finger on it because they smell and look like pretty much any other nursery. Their shrubs and trees are a bit pricey. But there's more. Most of their perennials come in small pint-sized containers, and are thus half the price of the larger nurseries. They have a few more unique plants, that's true, but not as many natives as I'd like.

The greenhouse is the nearest building to the parking lot, and the sliding door works only if you want in, not if you want out. That's either a great way to ensure customers or to break the fire code. Still, the venus flytrap method works.

Though it's a small green house, it still takes me a while to find what I came for because, well, you know how it goes. But there they are, liatris, then the agastache. Out back in the open, through the requisite and annoying main room full of birdfeeders and tacky statuary, I pick up a viburnum and an itea. Then I put them down. Surely nursery #1 has these cheaper, but why didn't I think about getting them there? Because I just realized I needed them. Look at them. They are perfect. Perfect.

Instead of hitting nursery #1 again, I can shoot down to its sister store on the south side of town, twenty minutes away, where their tree selection is the best. Might as well get some trees.

12 noon Nursery #3

The old man who works the tree and shrub lot out front greets me, asking if I need any help. No, I say confidently, admiring his straw hat and bypass pruners, one on each hip like six shooters. Of course, I have no idea where I'm going.

I walk up and down the rows and take thirty minutes to decide on one bald cypress of the ten I see. I've read up on how to choose, looking for a strong leader, no signs of stress in the bark, no infected branches. I like it here anyway, hidden by maples, oaks, birches, aspen, pine, crabapple, pear, willow…. Willow! Of course. Another twenty minutes and I've found a yellow-twigged willow, a cross between a black and weeping willow. How wonderful. I flag down the old man from across the lot. "Find something you want?" he yells from thirty feet away. "Yes, this tree here, and another over there." He asks me if that's all. Why'd he have to ask me that? I bet they have training sessions on how to ask questions, and on certain inflections and mannerisms which subliminally sucker in wide-eyed newbies like myself.

"Well," I say, "I'd like to get a viburnum and maybe an itea while I'm here." After red-tagging the trees, he leads me to the shrubs, where I select two before he asks, "Anything else for you today?" I head into the greenhouse and don't come out for half an hour.

1:30pm Nursery #4

Which is, technically, on the way back home from nursery #3, so I might as well stop in and check it out. They have the best sales and clearance, common stuff of course. I'm beginning to get most of my species plants from online nurseries, but shopping online isn't much of an experience. After rummaging through some things on sale under the large outdoor tent, I'm set for home. My trunk has two dozen plants that I'll likely dig within two days, and a truck will deliver two trees later this afternoon. But it won't keep me busy for long.

Sometimes, I come home feeling guilty. I didn't really need to buy so many plants, or even any plants at all. In later years

I'll visit a nursery just for the experience as my willpower grows alongside my full garden, which both grow inversely to my checking account. Still, there's always a plant or two. And when I return home I hide them behind a shrub, and sometimes plant them when I know my wife's in the shower or away at work. It's silly, I know she doesn't really care. But I know I have a problem. I know I need help. I have to get in as many plants over the summer as I can so they'll settle in over the winter. I'm always thinking ahead. Next week, I'll hit the same nurseries again, but I'll only get what's on my list.

Cassia hebecarpa – Wild Senna

Leaves like disks line each branch, prehistoric, some tropical fern, almost like a sensitive plant but that won't recoil to the touch. The bright yellow, pea-like blooms amass so many insects the four foot tall shoots seem to sag a bit more, from July to September as it flowers on and on. Furry white tongues reach from the centers of falling petals until each green seed pod grows six inches long, holding oval seeds in square compartments like some awkward pack of gum or medication. In fall, the peach-fuzz pods turn dark black, and the leaves a bright orange and rust. Cloudless sulphurs and silver spotted skipper caterpillars grow on the foliage, the skipper using its frass like a canon ball to defend itself. As the branches arc over the garden they cast a light shadow that lasts through winter, each a perch for a junco or goldfinch thinking hard about the seeds rattling just below.

Skin

My wife and I are standing in front of the bathroom mirror of a hotel in Columbus, Ohio. We've been married a month, and are attending a second wedding reception her parents are throwing, about 900 miles east of the first one we had the evening of our wedding in Nebraska.

"I can't believe you did this," she says. I can feel her breath against the skin of my back, almost as if I'd never felt it before. It's fresh, new, more tingly than ever. "Does it hurt?" she asks, standing behind me as I look wistfully into the mirror. "No," I say, "If anything it feels good, relaxing, calming even. A gentle message."

"You're like an onion." She reaches down to the waste basket then gets back to work, making occasional shuttering sounds. I can't believe she's doing this. Perhaps this is what marriage is. Peeling off the dead skin of your loved one after they burned their back gardening.

A week earlier I couldn't even sleep. For days the pain was unimaginable, and the vitamin E my wife spread on my back with a butter knife stuck me to my shirt, which stuck to the bed sheets. I just laid on my side and waited for morning, my back a billion tiny knives. What hurt the most, though, was knowing I couldn't go outside.

It was so hot that first summer. We were married when it was 105, and our evening reception on the prairie kept everyone inside the air conditioned building, lest our rented polyester clothes would melt to our skin. I gardened in 90 degree heat, 70 degree dewpoints, and like a man I'd never been before—dirty, sweaty, desperate for soil and sun—I ripped off my shirt and with machismo draped it over the copper obelisk. I wasn't thinking at all, I was on drugs, the natural chemicals in the soil spiking my endorphin level, the endorphin level making me feel invincible. I wanted a garden. Now.

My skin came off in neat sheets in Ohio, all the way from my shoulder down to my waste. I could sell this stuff like gold leaf to interior decorators, but more likely avant garde artists, like the ones who display rotting flesh with maggots in plexi glass boxes.

"Are you about done?" I ask my wife, glancing down to see the pile of skin like hair at a salon.

"Almost," she says. I can feel her nails picking at small, lingering pieces, once in a while grabbing hold of a skin vein and making one nice long peal. She's delightfully anal, and I could stand here all day purring like a kitten.

"That tickles," I say. "I'm surprised it doesn't hurt, I just can't believe that. It's so gross!"

"Then why are you doing it?"

"Because," she says smiling, "I love you." She wraps her arms around me, puts her face into my back, makes a spitting noise as if hair were caught in her mouth, then returns to scraping my back.

Dodecatheon meadia – Midland Shooting Star

The Perfect Hole

Nobody knows how to plant a tree. Not even the college kid, employed for the summer by a local nursery, who digs in my maple—the only tree of about fifteen I didn't plant myself. After trial and error of my own with other trees, it's clear the guy planted the maple too deep—I can't even see the root flare. Two summers later I tried to dig it up since it hadn't grown more than three inches, but the root ball was too massive, a few roots far down too stubborn. It took me four hours to figure this out, and I probably hacked apart most of the feeder roots.

At the grocery store mulch volcanoes spew out tree trunks in the parking lot's island plantings. Perhaps a foot of mulch is too deep. I don't know. Just maybe.

One of the first trees I dug in was a serviceberry. The hole was wonderfully wide, tapered perfectly to the undisturbed bottom, and the sides scarred by the tip of my shovel. I remember my wife coming out and complimenting me. But the hole was too deep and each year a new branch died back. I replanted it in the third year learning the hard way.

The second tree I dug in was a 12' river birch out in the open, full southern exposure in the lawn. I planted it 6-10" above grade and the thing died back to a few leaves the next spring—likely because I under watered it and put it in the wrong place. I cut back all the dead branches. Then I got on a flimsy ladder, and with an extension cord draped around my shoulder, used a jigsaw to take off half the dead trunk—this was before I bought a handy folding manual saw (in truth, a giant serrated switchblade, the same size as novelty combs you win at the State Fair). I moved the birch. Watered it like a fiend. Put down extra mulch since birch trees prefer shadier, cooler roots, and within a few months it had two feet of fresh growth. Voila.

In the late fall at a big box hardware store I rescued a 4' river birch. I called it my Charlie Brown birch, in honor of his scraggly Christmas tree. The thing was on its last leg, er trunk, but for $5 on clearance I had to try to save the young soul. After two years the tree is as tall, and wider, than the other birch I jigsawed in half.

A weeping bald cypress, also rescued from a big box for $20 on sale, grew from 4' to 8' in one year, then the next winter died back to the original 4'. I cut it in half and we'll see what happens. This may all sound like I don't know how to grow trees, but I'm learning the character of them. I think each tree has a personality, not only a genetic or environmental predisposition. Trees have a will to survive. On the verge of death they draw up every last reserve and produce a brilliant amount of seed. You'll see trees growing in rocky outcrops and on skyscraper roofs and out on a window sill cracks. Despite all our torture and general inhospitality, a tree will persist. That's certainly more than we can say for most summer-hired tree planters.

So I'm patient with the crabapple. Impatient with the bald cypress. Humbled by the river birch. Taught by the serviceberry like a forgiving grandfather. Some afternoons I get an urge to grab the spade and dig random holes, not just to feel the soil and breathe in the air or for the sunlight tanning my arms, but for the preparation, the hope, that if I learn to dig the hole right—even if it takes several hours—I'll be ready for the lessons that come after.

So much depends
upon

a wood
chip

glazed with fountain
water

beside the swamp
milkweed

I needed water in the garden, not only to fight back the hammering from new houses being built down the street, but for some potential wildlife. And, well, because water is fascinating to watch in any season. I grew up on a lake in Minnesota, one of those famed 10,000, and though I got motion sickness more than half the time, the way the water moved across the surface was the same as a flock of birds, a field of grass, a baseball game—all time and memory. I could stare for hours from the dock, into the shallows, and watch minnows scatter in front of a carp. In winter, the cool depth that could swallow you whole in a single gulp became Biblical in its ability to support you, your snowmobile, and eventually your car.

I stalked every nursery and trade show in town looking for a disappearing fountain. A pond was too big, too much work, I needed to approach water in baby steps after seeing my parents struggle—granted beneath a leafy canopy of maples—to maintain their own pond and a swimming pool.

There were plenty of fountains to be had, terribly expensive ones the size of bowling balls or shoe boxes. Seriously? And they all looked so fake, so mass produced. It made me wonder if anyone ever turned a garden gnome into a disappearing fountain and called it a day.

I contacted local landscape companies and found some guy with a field of boulders who would drill holes in said boulders. The drilling cost as much as a fountain at the nursery, which at least came with a basin and pump.

So I ventured to Omaha, settling on a mix of natural looking and mass produced—viva a cast concrete, mahogany-stained vase. After purchasing all the necessities it came to over $400. I could have purchased at least two trees for that price, but I've been told I already have enough trees.

I dug a square hole for the underground basin, carefully smoothed the hard clay bottom, even used a level to tweak the basin. A cinder block holds four square concrete steppers, which holds the fountain itself at over 3' tall. This intricate organization of materials took 7 hours, two trips to hardware stores, and much sawing of a plastic grate.

But the darn fountain still rocked, was still leaning, so that when I finally hooked up the pump all the water came down on only one side. I get some anal tendencies from my dad, and the older I get, the more anal I am, often reciting in my head "If you're gonna do it, do it once, and do it right." I can't tell you how many headaches I gave myself growing up, hearing those words from my dad, rolling my eyes far back into my skull.

But here I was. Such a central feature, right where the main garden path forked to two—slap darn in the middle of the garden—had to be perfect. I lifted off the fountain, rearranged the steppers, tried two cinder blocks, tried one, tried none, tried one again. I finally even lifted up the entire basin, emptying the water and checking the level again. It was all still perfect.

With the fountain rocking gently on the steppers it hit me that, well, maybe the fountain's base itself wasn't level. Perfectly obvious, but when a person gets so heated, involved, and well, perversely enraged at the hours passing by, it's easy to miss the smallest things. I wanted a fountain now. I wanted to bask in its splendor now. Yet, having a garden meant being patient and calm and open enough to notice only the smallest things, and I was learning this lesson the hard way, nature's way perhaps.

I looked around for something to shim the fountain. Coneflowers? Sedum? Birch tree? Fence?

Mulch, the garden's duct tape. I slipped in a few different pieces until I found the perfect one, and suddenly the fountain didn't move. The water slid down each side of the tall vase in gentle cascading sheets. It was a miracle, as if all that searching, all that time, were necessary for this one simple act. I remembered Shel Silverstein.

I laid down in the mulch, next to some milkweed and monarda, propped my head up with my arm and gazed at the water. It wouldn't be long before I caught robins bathing in the top, and butterflies sipping splashed drops from nearby stones. Every 3-4 days I have to refill it because of the Nebraska wind, and every 3-4 days I have to wait, stop in the garden, hold still in one place and see everything from a paused perspective—like the dead of winter, when water is ice, when the smallest sound or movement is amplified, and survival means holding fast to everything you learned in summer, yet unlearning it as you go.

Clematis virginiana in Early September

The Research Assistant Couldn't Experiment With Plants Because He Hadn't Botany

One time when my dad I were pulling out of a gas station, he stopped at the intersection to wait for traffic. I noticed the stop sign, several large cracks on its surface, and commented that someone must have said something funny. "What?" my dad asked. "Someone must have said something funny," I said, pointing to the stop sign. "It's all cracked up."

Most people don't get my subtle, "British" humor. Some say it's so subtle they don't realize the joke until hours later. Some say that doesn't make it funny at all, just sad. What I do know is that in a clay soil it takes a very long time to understand or "get" plants. I left for a week in early July, assuming everything was fine—everything looked fine—and came back to defoliated viburnums, absent perennials, a brown lawn, and faultlines in the garden. Absolute, bona fide, lose-a-wedding-ring-in-them cracks in the soil.

As I spread the mulch to reveal soil, or sidewalk paving, the network of cracks resembled a labyrinth of lightening bolts. I dropped a small pebble in one and couldn't hear it land. I pushed some loose soil into another and it never filled up. No matter what the garden looks like, established or not, if it hasn't rained for a week or two the sprinklers should come on for a few hours. Or, in clay soil, an hour on, two hours off, an hour on. I learned—by walking through a pond after watering—that clay soil isn't a very absorbent material.

The shock of these revelations was tempered, or exaggerated, by discovering that a faultline actually exists in Nebraska, and that this summer an earthquake around 3.0 or 4.0 hit eastern Nebraska. Whether the recent years of dry weather, or the draining of the Ogallala aquifer for farm irrigation, developed fault lines like the one on my garden is open to hyperbole and fantastical speculation. Either way, I know that when I garden the earth is always subtly shifting beneath me, hidden cracks tearing open into exposed root zones of new perennials I'm sadly losing. I haven't heard a good gardening joke in quite some time that might help relieve the stress and pressure of learning how to garden by trowel and error.

Hatchback Trees

No one stares. No one even looks over at the stoplight. I suppose that's fine, I don't want to make a scene. I'm just trying to get from point A to point B without losing too many leaves or side-swiping another car when I blindly change lanes.

The tallest tree I've had in my hatchback was an eight foot maple. The widest was about four feet, a weeping white birch 50% off at a big box store (it was too sophisticated for their usual clientele, I'm convinced, and thus its sale price). Since the tree was a weeper it went in easily, but came out like a child desperate to avoid the dentist.

Once a young man helping me asked if a tree would fit in my car. I laughed, scoffed, rolled my eyes and moaned a "duh." I folded down the backseats, lifted out the removable back dash, and my car suddenly became a self-propelled trailer that could comfortably fit a small cow. But there is a trick to hauling trees, and sometimes it does help to have someone up front threading branches through the front seats, past headrests, on to the dash, and out the window. I don't like coming home to find even one small twig has been torn off.

The pot is the biggest problem, like trying to lift a bag of shifting sand to your chest. Over the years I figure I've lost a good yard of planting medium, soil, mulch, and compost to my trunk.

I drive home at or below speed limit, taking the side roads, trying to reduce wind drag as the maple, birch, or crabapple needles its way out the passenger window. Often I'm poked and prodded along the way, twigs piercing my arm, my cheek, leaves tickling my ear, and once, a preying mantis taking the tree-bridge over into my hair and almost causing an accident. But I gave her a good home.

Maybe there's no art to hatchback tree hauling that makes me special. But I see kids in the backseat of a Ford pull up to a truck and whoop and holler at the black lab in the cargo bed, excitedly waving and barking, the dog wagging its tail like a windshield wiper on overdrive. I wish someone would pull up next to me, look over, smile, maybe even wink. Yes, I'd see them say in their eyes, yes, you are a man after my own heart.

2009

The satisfaction of a garden does not depend upon the area, nor, happily, upon the cost or rarity of the plants. It depends upon the temper of the person. One must first seek to love plants and nature, and then to cultivate that happy peace of mind which is satisfied with little.... If plants grow and thrive, he should be happy; and if the plants which thrive chance not to be the ones which he planted, they are plants nevertheless, and nature is satisfied with them.

— L.H. Bailey

Garden in 2009

650 Crocus Bulbs

Mid March, and there's a sea of yellow, white, purple and rust in the lawn. Winter is cut short, spring brought in early. Every little bloom nods in the breeze, lifted only a few inches above the putrid, dormant lawn. Everything is erased and rewritten. What I know is the shattering of darkness by the tiniest speck of light. On one bloom, near the willow, a honeybee has ventured out in the short rush of a warm, sunlit, late afternoon. Made brave, perhaps desperate, here in the bell of a white crocus the bee slides around the stamen like a moon in orbit, collecting the gravity well of life that maintains its equilibrium.

Late last fall, in a light mist, and in gloves and a wool coat, I let faith overwhelm me. I imagined the scene above in my dreams, and as the mail orders came in—vented bags full of skin-flaked bulbs—I could see so clearly the hope that March would be. Winter is spring, spring is winter. That hazy month of extremes would have hundreds of small anchors, reminding me from inside the house as a light snow fell, that nothing lasts, that I could shatter any boundary and remake the season. In fall I bent in cold grass and felt my numb fingers quit working—I didn't even notice when I cut myself. I stabbed at the hard soil with the tip of my sharp spade and pried open a crevice of earth, jammed a few bulbs into the clay, and tapped the lawn back down. I wound myself around the open space all day, busy, warmed at the core by this business. I wasn't a real individual with my own thoughts and desires, but something like a ghost dropping shadowed footprints across the landscape—pieces of me that would, in time, become something real.

Fire Pit / Bird Bath

As a wedding gift my parents gave us a fire pit to place on the back patio. We use it only a few times each year, since it's so good at catching rain water. This summer a frog used it as an afternoon oasis, much to the delight of our cats who enjoy sitting at the nearby window watching it leap in and out, as well as the birds coming for a drink. I also use it, on occasion, to douse burning mouse nests—sometimes I forget to check the gas grill before lighting it. So far, no roasted mice, though.

During the winter I put out a modest sixty watt bird bath heater in the fire pit / bird bath. With my cats I sit in the dining room at lunch looking through the sliding door. I stretch my bare feet into the sunlight, which reaches far into the house and across the wood floor, then briefly close my eyes, imagining that I'm standing in warm sand on some Mexican beach.

Suddenly, a bird I never see before lands at the fire pit in a frenzy of gold. It tip toes around the edge, looking down, hearing the water ripple in the wind perhaps, trying to find the best place to perch. It ruffles its wings and shows off a brilliant yellow underneath. Across its head on the back is a thin red band. He literally dances around the water's edge. One foot across the other, stepping side to side, like a supermodel walking down a ramp keeping her feet on one straight, imaginary line.

A few deep sips and it raises its head to drain the water down into itself, then lifts off into the trees a hundred yards away. I feel like I've been checked out, put on notice, made aware of something I can't comprehend. The northern flicker comes every few days during the winter, and maybe once a week in summer. With each year it seems another small piece is placed in the puzzle of my young garden, a spit of land that hasn't known such life for perhaps well over a century.

Colaptes auratus – Northern Flicker

Geum triflorum – Prairie Smoke

In fall the serrated rosette of leaves turns red at the tips, blushing or burning with the reflection of other falling leaves around them. Over winter a constant center of green remains, frozen in time as if seasons don't matter, that every moment is summer's apparition. The leaves lay flatter, one on top of the other, still furry smooth, like a bouquet of gathered blue jay feathers that are scattered around the garden. In spring new leaves burst forth like a dandelion, and in May short pink tails with a red droplet on the tip spike upwards. The tip opens, each filament glitters in the sun. Against your lips and nose, the bloom is like a troll doll's hair. With puffs of pink smoke a foot above the ground it's as if a fog has settled in places between larger plants, and as the haze clears, as the seed sets, as each follicle dries and loosens and finally lifts into the air, the green leaves remain as they always have—a center that holds the garden to its promise.

Mr. Mows All The Time

April 20, 2009

Mr. Mows All the Time is across the street. Not even May yet. And his yard is *maybe* 2/3 green, but more like 50%.

In his green shorts, grey tennis shoes, and straw hat—unbecoming for someone who's in his early 30s—he will mow 2-3 times per week until November. Rain or shine. Growth or no growth.

A few weeks after his first mow he scalps the yard, then for the next three days the yard will be littered with hoses as he tries to green up the damage. He will do this at least once every month. Sometimes his wife, with baby on hip, will have to move sprinklers in the early evening. No sprinkler remains on any portion of the lawn for more than thirty minutes.

Soon the chorus of mowers will drown out the spring birds gathering their nests, raising their young. When one mower stops, another will start up, as if keeping some sort of vigil, sentinels at the gate of tranquility that won't let you pass. In winter the snow blowers take over, but unlike their daylight cousins, snow blowers usually run at 6 or 7am. When I was growing up in Minnesota, a neighbor routinely did his driveway at 4am, just in time for the other neighbor to begin at 5am.

This winter Mr. Mows All the Time bought a snow blower.

April 19, 2010

Mr. Mows All The Time mowed this Monday morning, right on schedule. He mowed on Wednesday or Thursday of last week. It hasn't rained here in I can't remember how long. So, how much plutonium is he using to justify mowing twice a week, as he will do until hell or the lawns freeze over in November?

Yesterday my wife went to read on the garden bench in the morning. Read with an iPod even. She came in because our neighbor to the right began mowing his lawn.

Then as I was grilling dinner, the neighbor to the left

mowed her lawn.

Saturday morning I was grading essays at the kitchen table, and slid open the porch door to some lovely, purely miraculous weather. Within ten minutes the back neighbor comes plodding along on his riding mower—*wearing giant ear protectors* (like you'd see on aircraft carriers). What does that tell you? He had to mow his weeds, and I got to close the door and instead breathe my polluted indoor air.

This nonstop buzzing and whirling has me going insane. Two of my neighbors, including Mr. Mows All The Time, complete their 45-60 minute mowing cycles with blowing lawn clippings around. Mind you, we have 20-30mph winds quite often that cleanly and cheaply blow these clippings back on to the lawn. We live where wind comes sweeping down the plain like Armageddon.

Sometimes, I feel like the sooner we kill ourselves the better off the few of us left behind might be in the long run. That's a bad way to look at things, I know. Do people really enjoy mowing their lawn? Is this leisure time, connect with nature time, joie de vivre? What might they be escaping inside those houses? How much anger, fear, terror, and a sense of placelessness underlie all this mowing, all this rampaging about the landscape like Mr. Hyde?

As I pry apart the mini blinds to leer at Mr. Mows All the Time, I want to walk across the street with a sledgehammer and proselytize. But I'd rather have a natural conversation that segues nonchalantly to our discussing the 17 million gallons of annually-spilled gasoline, that lawn mowers alone (not including all those other unfiltered machines) comprise 5% of our nation's air pollution, and that walking behind a lawnmower your entire life greatly increases your chances for various lung diseases. I want to say that mowing for one hour puts out as much pollution as eight new cars driving highway speeds for the same length of time. I want to say, gee, Ryan, Jim, Steve, whatever your name is, all the synthetic fertilizer you spread four times each summer is a waste, and does nothing to improve the soil so you don't need to water or fertilize as much. You're just giving money to corporate drug dealers.

Then you know what I want to do? Like some Jehovah's witness I want us to be spiritually overwhelmed, get on our knees, and feel the grass. I want us to cry over all that spilled gasoline, all those petrochemicals leached into the dirt and our bodies—into the feet of his young son bouncing across the lawn—and I want a revelation. I want him to see his son light up chasing a bird that takes cover in a small street tree, or a butterfly hovering near a flower. I want him to connect the dots, and see the joy that this is, that one aster can save a bee colony, that one oak tree is host to over 400 different butterfly species alone. I want Mr. Mows All the Time to come to the dark side, because that's exactly where gardeners are—eccentric, hippy, go against the flow, crazy and insane plant nuts who you see piddling about in flower beds at dawn and dusk, likely practicing some kind of witchcraft, garnering a sinister earth-based knowledge that demands nothing less than a giant "A" be painted across their gardens.

I want this, but I know in my conversation I'd be too earnest, too direct, too opinionated. One must convert by example, even if it seems no one else is converting, so one must be patient. And one must do a lovely, gorgeous, subtly simple job of it—especially in the front yard. Someday, ages and ages hence, Mr. Mows All the Time might walk across the street and ask me about the weeping white birch, the fruiting dogwoods covered in robins, the chokecherry tree with red leaves. I might feel confident enough that he can handle the backyard, and gently nudge him around the corner, through the gate, and hope—as I always hope a passerby will do—get lost in the other world we've forgotten we're part of.

UPS, FedEx, USPS

For a homebody like me simple pleasures are gifts, more meaningful because I tend to stay put physically and psychologically. Cookies in the oven. A hummingbird at the sage. A monarch coming out of a chrysalis. An afternoon reading poems on a chair that was once my preferred spot as a child. When I wrote another book I did copious amounts of research, often buying cheap, used copies of books online so I could reread them at my own speed, write in them, dog ear, and enjoy them on the bookshelf like trophies. Every day a new package was in the mailbox, and every day I felt the echo of Christmas or a birthday, ripping open this gift, not sure what was inside, surprised that what I had asked for—or ordered—was now here in my hands. Books are so visceral and alive, their binding glue a smell like those cookies in the oven, warm and soothing; the rough paper inside like skin, my wife's skin, like pressed maple leaves or rose petals.

The only comparable joy to books in the mailbox is coming home after a long day of teaching to find a box or two on the front porch. Plants! Plugs and pint-sized plants, but plants nonetheless. Where are they from? Who sent them? How many are there? Oh, we must get them out and into the fresh air.

Online you can get anything from anywhere. I've even ordered from Amazon and Ebay. I once got a "tray" of 40 milkweed, test tube milkweed I called them—each plug was a bit smaller than I bargained for.

Every spring I get a box from Prairie Nursery and Prairie Moon Nursery—they are no relation to one another. Prairie Nursery packaging uses lots of rubber bands and green bamboo stakes to space the plants and keep them from launching up to the top of the box. Prairie Moon packs their plants as dormant bulbs and roots in plastic baggies with dog tag labels. The former has taught me that smaller plants establish faster than larger ones, and the latter that roots establish faster than small plants OR die faster because I still haven't mastered planting roots. In either case, without the shipments I'd have much less joy in my life, and far fewer native prairie plants, too. And the delivery men would be out of a job. In May there's a well-worn path from the street to my door through the front lawn.

I place my open boxes on the gardening chest on the covered deck, visiting the plants in the morning and evening as if they were patients recovering from surgery. I pace the garden, plan out what will go where. From the deck I stare transfixed for half an hour imagining the color, texture, and size of the mature plant in different positions. I use my thumb to size things up like I was taught in art class in high school. I pinch my fingers around a similar-sized plant in the distance and lift that invisible space over to another bed. A blue jay squawks from the top of the elm before diving for peanuts, leaping into the garden with two in his mouth, and tucking them into the soil beneath an aster. I hope nature prefers us planners.

The Naming

My wife and I are walking the garden after lunch. She comments on how thick everything is, especially in contrast to the picture I emailed her that morning, which showed the garden sprouting in April. After the annual cut down in March, the place is a moonscape—you could play a football game here unimpeded by any plant, except for a shrub or two. I often forget about the change that occurs, but when I stumbled upon that photo my jaw dropped. The garden is not a miracle, but it as close to one as I've ever witnessed.

My wife stops and says, "I mean, look at that." She nods toward the coneflowers and bluestem. "That was nothing just two months ago. I can't believe it."

I stoop to pull a weed and reply, "Yup, that's herbaceous perennials for you. Pretty amazing."

She looks down to me with a quizzical look, as if I'd just stammered, or started speaking in French. "What kind of perennials?"

"Herbaceous," I say, "perennials that come from the ground up every year." She turns back to look at the coneflowers and a moth landing on an early bloom.

"Her-bay-shus" she says slowly, as if rolling a piece of candy around in her mouth. "Her-BAY-shus," she says again, but putting more emphasis on that stressed second syllable.

"Are you ok?" I ask.

"Yes. I just like the way it sounds. Her-BAY-shus." She says it this time a bit more sensually, like you might say "curvaceous" as you slide your hands down your body parallel to one another, imagining the form of a perfectly sculpted supermodel.

"You're weird." I say, staying on my knees, reaching into plants for more weeds I'm now noticing. She ignores me, and with the delight of a new word still pulsing through her, asks what a tall plant is.

"Eupatorium," I respond, looking up then looking back down quickly, getting lost in my work as I do too often, the garden an impossible siren song I can't ignore.

"Yew-pa-tor-ee-ummmm," she says, letting the last consonant hum through her and echo, ricochet through her bones. "YEEEEW-pa-TOR-eeee-uumm." The second time is more playful, a quick "Yewpaw" and a long "toreeum." She says it again, and it reminds me of watching Sesame Street, with the words on the bottom of the screen and a ball bouncing along on each syllable as it's spoken. Somehow, this comforts me.

She starts walking again around the garden, on her own now, completing a circuit that often takes her no more than ten minutes, and can take me anywhere from thirty minutes to a few hours. Soon, she's sitting on the bench, staring off into the distance, then the sky as several franklin's gulls circle west overhead. I get up and stoop a dozen times, pulling weeds, noticing insects, calculating when something will bloom. I can see my wife on the bench mouthing the words I've taught her, sometimes looking at me, sometimes a plant. Each sound is a concrete thing like the perennials, but also as abstract and ephemeral as a summer afternoon seducing you to stay a while longer.

Echinacea purpurea – Purple Coneflower

Deadheading Grasshoppers

Globe thistles are like mirror balls, or marbles, or that crystalline spacecraft the infant superman crash landed in. They are beautiful and unique blooms, and pollinating insects favor them. The only issue is their dangerous leaves, so placing the tall plant in the back of a bed is important--unless you don't like others to visit your garden.

Well, maybe there are two issues with the plant. After days of admiring my blue and white globes, watching bees push pollen on to their back legs, I awoke to find the majority of the foliage gone. Maybe this isn't a problem, unless you enjoy perennials—which I do.

Some of the thistle leaves look skeletonized, others are just gone. What could do this? I made my move to look closer, placing one foot carefully between the coneflowers, liatris, and thistle, and a swarm of fifty grasshoppers leap like a flock of sparrows from the cover of switchgrass and sunflowers.

Within a week not only were the thistles defoliated, but so were several other young plants just trying to get a toe hold in their new soil. I read up on everything grasshopper, how this year was the worst in some time, how if you kept areas around the garden unmowed or otherwise tall that might hold back the insects. I read about cilantro and other plants that could work as barrier crops, ran to the nursery, bought a dozen, planted them, and things only seemed to get worse.

The trick, it would seem, is to get the grasshoppers as young nymphs. Sometimes, soapy water works, but it's really not proactive enough. Semaspore bait seemed to be the key, and theoretically only affected grasshoppers. But it was July. I need to get the adult grasshoppers, especially the females—soon I'd catch them with their abdomens stuck down into the soil laying eggs.

I didn't know what to do. I'm a mother hen when it comes to the garden, staking partially torn twigs or flower stems, placing supports in spring anticipating the floppy growth in summer, caging young plants from rabbits, lifting ladybugs to where the aphids are (like they didn't have a clue). You name it, not much escapes my eye. I wasn't going to lose any plant, not a one, to the forces of nature. Besides, I convinced myself, grasshoppers aren't nature, they are a hell-sent plague—they need a good winnowing down.

Truth be told I was enraged. Chemical sprays weren't an option. I was thinking organic, but nothing organic worked, including pepper and garlic sprays (I think that simply spiced up the greens like salad dressing). Organic. What's organic. Something relatively benign to the ecosystem. And something that makes me see the results, feel the results.

One evening after dinner I was deadheading some coreopsis, moving my fingers and scissors delicately between the small blooms and thin wiry stems, thinking to myself how easy it would be to slice a finger in half. So easy. The more I thought about it, the more I was sure I'd do it.

Clinging vertically to one stem was a grasshopper. I need to deadhead anyway, so without a second thought I cut through the grasshopper and stem together. Two birds with one stone.

But wait. Is that ethical? Scissoring a grasshopper like that? It split so cleaning, so delightfully, so easily. Neither half seemed alive. It was painless, right?

It was liberating. Look. Another grasshopper. And another. Two down. They seem to prefer hiding in the grasses. Five. Ten. Twenty. I followed them around the garden, into the ironweed and eupatorium, around to butterfly bushes, back to the bluestem. The snip snip sound of the scissors was so crisp, so fast and permanent. It felt good, that echo of the shears pulsing through my hand up into my arm. Snip snip. Thirty. Forty. I was saving the garden, the neighborhood, Nebraska. Fifty. Sixty. Snip.

It's not easy though. You have to approach from behind. I'd angle in the opened scissor through stems and blooms, and quickly clamp down on the body. Sometimes I took a flower—a cardinal sin because I won't even let my wife cut a few flowers for the house. Other times I could get two at once, and one time I got two while mating. Their mating. I could never master chopsticks, but this, this I could perfect if I gave it enough time. It felt diabolically zen.

For days I scissored grasshoppers. It was perhaps the most relaxing endeavor in the garden I'd ever experienced. And I'm fully aware of the carnage, the irony of a native wildlife gardener, a lover of insects, life, and the pursuit of happiness. After my wife caught me in the act she yelled at me, even cried, saying how terrible a person I was then stormed back into the house. She made me swear not to scissor grasshoppers again. And I swore. I didn't do it again. But I wanted to. I came so close.

Sitting on the bench I feel something land on my back, it's prickly legs tugging on my shirt as it gets a better hold. I jump up and fling the grasshopper to the ground, watching it leap off to some perennial I knew was a goner. Tooth and claw, a gardener must learn, and let the garden do and be what it will. It isn't really mine, anyway—which is perhaps the hardest lesson a gardener may ever learn.

The King is Dead, Long Live the King

The preying mantis is upside down on the culvers root. One arm is feeding the body of a bumblebee to its vice-grip jaws, the other cradles the bumblebee's head in the elbow. The head is still moving.

Another mantis is near the top of a butterfly bush, but with the head of a skipper butterfly completely missing. Both arms are holding the winged body like a corn cob.

Carnage is good for a garden. The decay and death rebuild the soil, smother weeds, create homes for all kinds of insects and amphibians. I'm always stunned when people respond to my mantis stories by covering their ears, because I know that without those stories, without the mantis, I'd have a very poor garden. The more that is devoured, the more evidence of life changing hands, the more I know that I've helped start a thriving ecosystem. The satisfaction a mantis has after stalking its prey, lunging and capturing, is the same fulfillment I feel. I am nourished by a headless bumblebee, through memory and story, and the thin line that separates its fate from my own. We both come from the soil, and indeed are soil, only given temporary reprieve from its confines.

Parthenium integrifolium – Wild Quinine

With large leaves reminiscent of melting hacksaws, stalks rise several feet in late spring to bloom through summer. Each white flower is a small, cauliflower pentagon—not really a flower, as one thinks of in a garden, but a sponge or some sort of perfectly-shaped, fizzing snowflake. The insects don't mind, coming often and staying a while. From a distance the tips of each floret look like a joe pye weed. In fall the blooms turn russet, easy to pinch and toss like beans, though hardly any will come to much. If a season were to be transported to another, winter would sit here, atop the quinine, and cast out a frosted glance from behind the coneflowers and black-eyed susans. There are ghosts, one knows, that have broken through fevers of drought and fire and plow—to gingerly settle undisturbed, at peace again, as it was in the prairie, the old country.

Ambergate Gardens

Every summer I visit my parents in Minnesota. Every summer I have to find some way to fit four or five cardboard trays of plants into my car, along with the suitcases and other things.

My mom and I will visit a few nurseries, some she's been waiting months to hit until I come north. Our favorite place is at Ambergate Gardens, which is simply a field of flats, a roundabout of plants centered around a pile of mulch. The nursery is down a bumpy dirt driveway, through an open field, around a pond and through the trees, then into a small clearing of many native Plains perennials. Most every pot is infested with weeds, and the owners pick out every last one when you bring them to the pitched party tent at the far end, next to a parked truck with a generator running inside. It almost feels like a fly by night operation, some sort of carnival, except they are firmly entrenched on an acreage surrounded by large suburban homes itching to develop this last bit of land.

Since we come every year, the owners ask me how school is going, what I'm writing, do I know the owners of a nursery in Lincoln that they like. We talk about gardening, ecology, or politics as they keep potting and sorting seedlings on trays behind them. We easily spend an hour or more here just browsing, stooping over to read plant tags, the sun on our backs, the call of geese in the pond rushing over us. The owners themselves are incredibly tanned and freckled, his beard bleaching a white gray, her hair bleaching even whiter. When we talk about my book, my dissertation, my mom says that I even mention them, to which I get an astounded laugh and then a hearty thanks, and we talk about books they've published on northern perennials.

My mom and I will pull our red wagons over the rutted mulch roundabout, load up, and sigh deeply at the welcomed rush of air conditioning from the car's air vents. "I wish you came back more often, so we could come to Ambergate," my mom says. I agree. She proposes a late lunch, but I don't feel hungry anymore. I'm pleasantly full, feeling the day pulse then settle through me like a Thanksgiving dinner followed by homemade chocolate pie. I could pass out contentedly and dream the garden like never before.

New Model Year

Gardens are like cars. Go with me on this. You've got your Cadillac gardens, massive beds, large scale parterres and fountains, prim and proper. But there's the Japanese or Zen style gardens, er, I mean Toyota Prius—never assuming, but quiet, peaceful, socially connected to the larger world and landscape around it. You've got you Fords and GMs, you know, foundation plantings from a bix box nursery, whatever came with the house. Then there's those exotic plants you shouldn't have, that have no business in that environment, that can't even handle snow and need too much pampering and cost far too much in the first place, but they sure are nice to salivate over—Bugatti, Astin Martin.

Then you've got gardens that are like a 1985 Honda CRX or some other small, two door car that just won't quit. It's rusted, beat up, smells like every restaurant and air freshener imaginable, it doesn't get you out of the city, but what it lacks in dependability and sex appeal it makes up for in decent gas mileage and readily-available parts on Ebay. This kind of garden comes from Home Depot, and usually looks like an under-watered, scraggly maple marooned in the front yard, with some boxwood hugging the house, and in the fall some geraniums in a pot or two, (doped up with Miracle Gro).

Finally, you've got your minivan gardens. I'll call them vegetable beds. Completely utilitarian and economical, practical. But there's always a new scratch, a new ding, something spilled on the carpet. There's always a head of lettuce missing, infested tomatoes, strawberries pecked to death by birds. But you're not in it for the now, you're in it for the long haul. The experience. The nurturing. The hope that what you provide will create a better future. Vegetable gardens seem more altruistic to me, maybe like that Toyota Prius.

Still, who doesn't dream of that sexy something sitting next to you in the Maserati convertible, both of you perfect, complete because of your fortune 500 company or the sweet inheritance or the lawsuit against Monsanto that actually stuck once hell froze over. Look at you two, wind in your luscious hair, dressed in Armani, sipping champagne from the refrigerator glove box—like some modern day Louis XIV strolling down Versailles as groundskeepers rush ahead to turn on fountains just for you.

Dragonfly

Sometimes I feel Jurassic, or Pre Cambrian. Sometimes I feel swarmed, overwhelmed, made small by the dark shadows below which are far larger than the thing which made them. I suppose this is like memory, something that morphs and grows much larger than it originally was.

During hot summer days dragonflies buzz the garden. Sometimes three or more at a time. In perfect ovals they pace the sky about fifteen feet off the ground, diving and rising like subtle roller coasters as they skim mosquitoes. Their long wings are inaudible, unimaginable. At dusk a dozen glue themselves to the west side of the fence, taking in every last moment of sunlight and warmth.

A dragonfly perches on the very tip of the topmost liatris bloom. The pink marbled bulb has yet to open, and though the insect seems precarious in the wind, those thin dragonfly legs latch on easily. Not one part of the dragonfly shutters or moves, not even the wings catching a sudden gust, wings that in their stillness seem to be navigating the air as if in perfect flight. The whole garden is that much more calm and assured, even as perennials bend and tangle into one another. I'll wait with the dragonfly and be made smaller by the ancient shadow resting in this place.

Dragonfly on Liatris Bud

Liatris ligulistylis – Prairie Blazing Star

August is pouring down heat, is thick with humidity, is raining monarchs. On five foot spikes the blooms zigzag, stagger, step up the long ladder of growth, each flower placed in such a way that it might accommodate dozens of butterflies at once. The bright purple petals spill from their centers, fifty or more, each licking the air with undetectable scents. One monarch erratically hovers then lands. Another. Another. Finally a half dozen at once until something shakes them, stirs them up into the air, each making a wide circle of the garden and slowly spiraling in back toward the blooms. This is the perfect time of year, the last of the monarchs emerging, readying for their exodus south. In two months puffs of seed will spill from the places where the blooms were. Blow on them like a dandelion. Each seed takes flight, a butterfly's shadow, released from the earth to be sheltered by it again in some place that will echo this one.

I Succumb to You, Autumn, Like a Memory

The morning glories have died. Their stems and leaves are wilted and limp this morning. The bright green of those heart-shaped leaves is a mass of forest green, nearly a rich black soil--of which they will now become.

It was not a hard freeze, but it was another thirty degree night. At 11pm I almost went outside to cover them, as I did two weeks ago, but I was tired. I wanted to give in to my body after a long day, a long week. I wanted sleep. It was time to let go.

I move my hand into the damp silk of foliage, no longer careful like I was yesterday when hidden bumble bees would emerge like candle smoke from the long throats of blooms. In the wind I let one leaf rest on the back of my hand until it lays flat. It is like my grandmother's hand. Clammy, limp, tired, and ready to say something final we don't need to say--the touch is a thousand words, a synapse that fires from neuron to neuron and passes on the memory. And the memory of memories.

Each spring it takes me longer than I'd expect to start morning glories. I plant unique varieties after soaking the seeds overnight. I wait for fourteen days. Nothing. I soak and plant again. I wait fourteen days. A leaf, like a mushroom, here and there. I wait for the vines to wake slowly, as they always do, a millimeter a day. Then an inch. Then one day a foot or three. Which plant will it be?

But the only morning glories that bloom are self-seeded 'Grandpa Ott,' the same dark purple as last year. No chocolate or white, no blue. But they come. The vines come like an olfactory sense and cover the deck railing, then hide the deck, the window, shade a part of the wall. Butterflies pupate in the deep, thick shadows. Tree frogs shelter from afternoon sun. A preying mantis feasts on a skipper, its body parallel to a thin, curled shoot diving out into the negative space of air and sky.

The morning glories have died. The birch leaves are down. The amsonia is sunlight unto itself. The shadows of cedars cover half the garden. The asters are a week gone. Nothing is left, yet everything is here, still, dug in and waiting. Like the purple morning glory seeds I planted only once, years ago, and that will come again in May. I'll wait. I give myself to the winter now so that I might earn the spring and come into the balance of seasons, and if I'm lucky, myself. I remember my mother's morning glories. She remembers her grandmother's. And so the morning glories remember us all.

2010

To live in this world
you must be able
to do three things:
to love what is mortal;
to hold it

against your bones knowing
your own life depends on it;
and, when the time comes to let it go,
to let it go.

— Mary Oliver

Garden in 2010

Rapture

The juncos have been feasting at the feeders this winter, dozens at a time, stopping first in shrubs to make sure the coast is clear, then leapfrogging like checkers toward the open yard. Sometimes the entire flock will jolt into the air and run for cover, and for five minutes the space is empty and silent. Then one junco will venture out, land on the ground, peck at the seed-covered snow. Then another. Then thirty—until they get spooked again.

I'm sitting on the couch, flipping between a television show on U.S. air tactics in the first Gulf War, and an episode of Airwolf. Out of the corner of my eye I see a swoop of a large bird, a streak of white and olive. A flicker?

I race to the sliding door and can't see anything. Nothing at the feeder or birdbath, nothing at the suet. I scan the tops of trees. Nothing. I look between the skeletons of perennials and don't see anything move, not until a stroke of dark brown tail feathers pulse from behind the base of the arborvitae. A small hawk quickly lifts from the ground, junco in its clutches, and vanishes into the tree line.

I slip on my shoes to inspect the battlefield, astonished that this happened right here, in my tranquil haven—that nature, in all its forms, has come here to roost so fully. I find only a few scattered grey feathers, some in the folds of dark green thuja, some in the snow, but not a trace of blood. It was a clean kill, something with skill and even honor. Such terror in a moment, it seems wrong to be here, out in the cold, painting a picture of awe and rapture.

The Geese, The 50, The Iris, The Waiting

This morning I opened the sliding door to scare away two squirrels at the bird feeders. I was angry. I'd put out a nutty squirrel log to distract them, but they aren't distracted yet. Didn't matter. Nothing else in the world matters when, after 40" of snow (average is 20") and three months of a very cold winter, a person opens a door at 10am in early March and.... Spring. My god it's spring. Standing in shorts and a t-shirt in bright sun and a light wind, it's spring. I wanted to shout it. I wanted to call back to the massive hordes of geese honking back and forth to one another like a game of marco polo. I want in. I am in.

Fifty degrees never felt so real. It was a full immersion, a blessing, a baptism that slides right through your skin, muscle, veins, and blood. By the birch, iris reticulata pokes up out of the ground like fresh bamboo shoots. In the garden the snow is melting fast now, water pools in the bottoms unable to penetrate the frozen clay soil. The grasses, the sedges, the asters—these are all now emerging from the snow flattened like bed hair. The only winter interest the garden has this year was a continuous one foot of wet, heavy snow ripping off large branches of chokecherry and viburnum that will take years to regrow.

Maybe it's spring. Maybe it's not. I've been tricked before, I've let myself fall in love with moments and thoughts too often not to be a little realistic, a little jaded. Morning. It sounds too much like mourning. And yet I've also discovered that the opposite of a thing is often that thing—that what is, isn't, and so more truthfully is. Mourning is morning, the beginning of a recovery.

Spring. A coil tightly wound, compressed flat to the earth, all that stored and hidden energy, all that promise and hope, all that electric, faster-than-light, in-the-blink-of-an-eye potential and change just waiting. A trap. A rabbit hole. A rock at the top of a hill.

Hundreds of geese this morning ride the wind northwest. Iris reticulata spikes the air. Fifty degrees echoes back to December first and the fall garden. My bare legs on the back steps are like roots, tree leaves, taking in the morning again as if seasons never existed and I am the first one to know this world.

Pulsatilla vulgaris – Pasque Flower

In April fingered leaves reach up like praying hands, and from their centers an oval of dark magenta rises covered in peach fuzz. The stem too, thick and short, seems to be covered in a white halo, as if emerging from a bed of frost. The thin petals unfurl, dark purple, at the center a gumdrop of yellow stamens. And there, at the center of the center, a wild explosion of purple like a frozen mushroom cloud, the style, an echo of the flower's rising, the petals unfurling. Everything about this is chilled, preserved, a bridge between the cold nights and suddenly warm days. Every new bud breaking ground seems awkward and unsure, even premature. They keep low, careful to not leave the safety of the warming soil. In the evening the only sign that there was a flower is the gathering together of soft tentacles to preserve the next day's resurrection.

Fetch

After dinner in summer is the only time, except morning when I'm asleep, when the garden cools down enough to be tolerable. Searching for the solitude I thrive on, the silent explorations and discoveries in the garden, I make my circuit with a pruner in one hand, and a Hershey bar in the other.

Wherever I go I disturb life. Butterflies feeding, grasshoppers mating, moths resting, frogs climbing the fence, birds hiding in the dense perennials. And I'm sure there's life I can't even perceive that I displace, that I even kill. I'm careful, though, as I walk by plants I know have larvae crawling on them, like the milkweed and baptisia. A few spiders run from the centers of their webs, even after a fresh kill, and burrow in to folded-over leaves where they keep their egg sacs.

The blue willow shrub by the fence is in need of constant trimming because I can't stand to make it smaller. I like its natural girth, and the viceroys lay their eggs on it. But it has simply become too big for this spot, encroaching on the bridge over the dry stream bed and path, so I begin careful removal of a few stems. I step back to see it's lopsided, try to make it appear natural, open up the middle to sunlight, step back, try again. I don't really know how to prune.

I hear my neighbor's sliding door open and close, and his big black lab come pouncing through their yard with his dog tag clanging like obnoxious wind chimes. The neighbor whistles, yells something, and I hear an object hit the fence a few feet from me. I try my best to ignore it, but the moment, the evening—what I needed after a stressful day—has all been obliterated. I know I've lost something I won't find again.

To me, being in the garden is much like writing. When I'm in the moment, I can't type fast enough, and sometimes this means I lose trains of thought that popped into my head. Where would they have taken me? I assume somewhere surprising and invigorating, since that's usually the case. If the doorbell rings, or I hear my cat licking plates on the counter until they fall to the floor, I lose momentum and I can never slide back into that place where I left off. It's impossible. Frustrating. Completely deflating.

My neighbor whistles again, and I hear his dog come panting and jingling toward me. I wonder if this guy knows I'm here, inches on the other side of the fence—my fence that I paid for and that he enjoys for free. I wonder if he knows how annoyed I am, how quickly I get angered, how without the garden I think I might, on certain days, lose myself to some rage I feel in my genes.

A raggedy, chewed up, dismembered toy comes falling six feet in front of me. I've found tennis balls and other toys before, and once two tennis balls held together by a piece of rope—some medieval-looking device that deadheads swaths of blooms in one throw.

I walk over and toss the toy back over the fence. "Sorry about that!" I hear from the other side. I stew. It seems he did know I was here. Or worse, discovering I'm here now, his apology seems half-hearted, not enough. "It's cool," I yell back, wishing I could freeze them both with a stun gun. I tell myself that if I see broken blooms, I'll say something. On other evenings they'll toss tennis balls against the fence for ten minutes at a time. They have an uncanny ability to begin mowing just as I come outside, and the garden wreaks of an oil refinery while sounding like a jet engine. Sometimes when I'm weeding, I'll toss bits over the fence just because I can. Often, I'll let my dandelions blow that way, I mean, I'll blow them that way.

I know I'm petty and mean, and that I should get over it. Life's too short. Let bygones be bygones. Recite a platitude and feel better, cover it up, let it stew and compost. Or passive-aggressively plant more perennials along the fence. No one ever got hurt planting flowers.

Dogfighting

I've been in the garden for an hour now, sitting on the bench or crouched behind indian grass and boltonia. I have my SLR camera slung over my neck, the 200mm zoom fully extended and ready. I point to the sky, take the picture again and again, hoping to get just one good image.

The majority of the pictures are a slate of blue, some simply a white haze. In one, on the bottom right corner, is a blur of orange, something escaping the view. I'm frustrated. Sure, this isn't an easy task, but I've been waiting, I've been snapping up photos like potato chips, and still I can't translate this event into something tangible. I can't share it with anyone.

The monarchs twist and slide across the sky, their double helix going both vertical and horizontal, completely 3rd and—it seems at times—4th dimensional. Where'd they go? Suddenly they appear on the other side of the garden like leaves caught in an updraft. I assume one is male, the other female, he trying to tire her out and get her on the ground. For the first time a few weeks ago I caught a couple on the eupatorium 'wayside,' an hour later they'd landed in some iris, their abdomens stuck together like a Chinese handcuff.

Today the two monarchs in the air split off, and one dives towards another nectaring on some liatris, and off they go into the air, until splitting and repeating the same collision with other monarchs in the garden. It seems like a restless life I can't imagine.

After trying a myriad of positions, I finally get one picture, but when I bring it inside it's blurry. Still, the two butterflies seem to be facing off, a dual, but more like a scene from Crouching Tiger, Hidden Dragon. I see only one form in an intricate, chaotic chorus whose moves and positions must be as infinite in design as a snowflake or fingerprint. Those four wings might be pushing and pulling the air in four different ways, all at once, without a second thought, just instinct, nature in its purest form.

I come back outside after dinner to try again, but I can't get anything. I am slow and lumbering, my finger on the shutter inadequate, my marvel of technology hardly any better. All I can do is sit here, with the camera set down beside me on the bench, and burn this moment into my brain: the warm air smelling of mountain mint, the sun on my back, the summer flowers in full bloom about to transition into autumn and seed, the monarchs coming closer, then landing beside me.

Monarch on Asclepias incarnata

Danaus plexippus

In the spring of 2008 I planted one or two swamp milkweed. I read somewhere that it's the preferred host for monarch butterflies. And although I knew what a monarch butterfly looked like, I wasn't entirely sure I'd ever seen one.

Over the 2008 growing season I must have planted at least 100 different perennials of various sizes. In all of this chaos and hunger, I forgot about some of them, like the milkweed. I knew it'd be years before I saw any kind of significant wildlife, so I never looked closely at my small plants.

But one day I paused at the milkweed. It looked infested. That's how I was raised—any plant that had a bunch of things crawling on it was infested, and needed a good insecticidal spray. I must admit, for a moment I thought about this, not having fully immersed myself in the idea of organic gardening—or that something with purpose was beginning on those leaves.

The more I looked, the closer I got, a dozen or so fat and juicy caterpillars didn't seem entirely evil. Watching them move from leaf to leaf, occasionally sliding out frass as nonchalantly as the birds flying over my newly-washed car, I was enamored. Then it hit me—these must be monarch caterpillars. A revelation!

After some images online I confirmed it. Amazing. Right here, in a very bare and blazing open space with a few twigs sticking out of two thousand square feet of mulch, there was a colony of thriving monarchs. Within a week or two I counted as many as 30 plump caterpillars crammed on to just two milkweeds. My planting slowed to a creep. I spent more time watching the monarchs then doing anything else. One day I spent two hours following a few escapees all around the garden—I figured they were crazy, lost, and put them back on the milkweed. They had crawled ten feet in only a few minutes, over all kinds of terrain. Looking back, I didn't realize just how naïve I was about gardening and nature. Here I was, 31 years old, writing environmental essays and poetry—gardening all the while—and I knew nothing.

That began to change when I brought in a few caterpillars, placing them in an old two gallon aquarium that once raised baby guppies. If you've never watched a caterpillar turn into a chrysalis, let alone emerge from one, you are leading a diminished life. I took picture after picture, video after video, it was far better—and less destructive—then bringing in flower cuttings. After two weeks we had a few healthy butterflies to release, and in 2009 we raised about fifty monarchs and a dozen black swallowtails. Some of those swallowtails came home from the nursery on some parsley and fennel. Ok. I picked them off of other plants and had about eight on one small plug. The cashier commented "Oh my, looks like you have some hitchhikers." Whatever she thought was fine by me as I long as made it out the door.

In 2010 I went on to Craig's List and bought a used ten gallon aquarium from a young girl who, with her older brother, met me in a McDonalds parking lot. It felt like a drug deal. Over the summer and winter we raised almost 200 monarchs, thirty swallowtails, and several pints of feces. I cleaned the aquarium almost daily, then learned I didn't clean it well enough. Monarchs spread a parasite known as OE, and it can lead to caterpillars who convulse, go limp, and die trying to turn into a chrysalis, and others that emerge coated in a black oil that deforms their growth. I started bleaching my containers, spending thirty minutes a day caring for almost ten separate containers. I had a monarch assembly line Henry Ford would admire:

Container #1 – Monarch eggs on leaves. Other monarchs eat right through the eggs as they munch on leaves, and caterpillars at any stage can get infected by the tachnid fly. The first time you see a caterpillar about to turn into a chrysalis, hanging dead, with silk threads dangling out like commando zip lines from a helicopter, you feel something isn't right. Until you see the tachnid fly larvae wobbling around below—then you know.

Container #2 – 3 day old caterpillars the size of, well, very hard to see.

Container #3-6 – Larger caterpillars.

Containers #7-9 – Monarchs ready to be chrysalides in the big aquarium.

My wife made the mistake of encouraging me after we discovered the plight of monarchs—how milkweed is considered a noxious weed and its stands are far and few between; about the incredible 3,000+ mile monarch migration from as far as southern Canada to central Mexico each fall; about the vanishing forests turned into firewood or cultivation, forests that protect the overwintering monarchs each year, and the climate change that is also contributing that will make the region inhospitable by around 2050.

In the end, though, everything comes down to size. Though I will never raise as many monarchs again, all the matters of the world, the cultures, the environments, and tooth and claw existence we all share, everything comes down to this simple creature that holds so much resonance, that transcends everything, that binds it all together.

I watch a monarch butterfly drop out of its now clear chrysalis, its wings begin to move, all smaller than your pinky finger nail. Its proboscis unfurls and curls, its feet grasp for better leverage, knowing that if it falls it might damage its fragile, young wings. In ten minutes the wings are half inflated, in another ten they are full and ready to air dry. How did all of that fit into such a small space? How did an egg, the shape of a bullet and the size of a sesame seed, become this? How did I become who I am?

In a few hours the monarch is scratching at the walls of its enclosure, flitting around, banging into what it must perceive as invisible force fields. Placing it on my finger it tickles like a spider, and for a moment I feel as if it may as well be a giant raptor about to take flight. And when it does, this not-so-fragile insect— that weighs as much as a paperclip—lifts into the wind like it has known nothing else, never been anything but flight, and every sorrow, pain, and joy falls to the side as trivial and petty concerns of our own overactive imaginations.

Favorites

As a writer and English teacher, I'm asked by everyone who can speak what my favorite book is. I abhor that question. I have only three bookshelves in my office, all overflowing, and I need at least three more to get all the other books off the floor, out of the closet, unpacked from boxes.... I stand there, among all these books, and remember moments.

Frankenstein takes me back to a summer in high school when the book was required reading over break, and I was so upset about having summer homework I never read it, and failed a test early that fall. There's *Jane Eyre*, and a girl's hand on my knee during class. There's *Letters to a Young Poet*, which began an overindulgence in Rilke early in college. Then there are books I used for research, things on garden design, landscape history and philosophy, and ecology and nature. Poems and memoirs and novels and short stories like fingerprints. So many. Which one is my favorite?

As a gardener I'm asked by everyone who can speak what my favorite plant is. I can take you out to almost any plant in the garden and tell you its story: where I bought it, how it's grown, what insects or animals are attracted to it, what color it gets in fall.... Which one is my favorite?

At the garden gate is a crabapple which flowers clouds of pink and whose leaves our burgundy in spring, then turn dark greenish / red in summer. It watches over the garden entrance, looks down the entire length of the garden, and is a broadening canopy that hints at the peace and seclusion beyond.

In 2010 a little filipendula plena finally bloomed. This plant gets fern-like ground foliage, then shoots up a few stalks a foot into the air with delicate blooms on the end that smell exactly like the crabapples which bloomed months before.

Asters.

The subtle smokey blooms of a purple-flowering baptisia, whose leaves are also a subtle smokey blue.

Liatris.

Wild senna.

The black-eyed susan that gets six feet tall with blue,

cabbage-like leaves.

Dogwood.

The feathery amosonia that turns bright yellow, then a bright rust in October.

The milkweed whose seeds lift off into the air like puffs of winter breath.

The spiraea I drove forty minutes one way for, and just the spiraea.

What is your favorite plant? I stand over the catalog of the garden, looking out from the deck, each bloom and leaf like a book's spine, bringing back moments, feelings, sensations beyond touch, sight, or smell. The garden speaks to me, rocks me to the core, tears me open and rebuilds me carefully and confidently into its own image. There is no separation, no way to quantify such transformation and fusion with a question or its answer. My favorite plant is.

Tall Plants

It's not because I have a bad back or rickety knees, but I just prefer to look my plants in the eye. I don't like looking down at them—you can't see their world. And besides, everyone has flowers that are one to three feet high, so what? Of course, landscape folk will say put the tall perennials in the back of the border, to which I scoff before I yawn with boredom. Every time I visit a botanical garden it's the same thing over and over and over—same colors, same plants, same design.

I put a six foot eupatorium right at the curve of a path, so it blocks the view around the bend a little but while nudging you into the curve as your elbow grazes it. I've got some monarda fistulosa at eye level and near the path so you can both smell the leaves and actually hear the bees—sight is over privileged in the garden, and most art forms, too. There's five foot sage arcing over into the path daring you to nectar like a hummingbird (go ahead, no one's watching). Tall coreopsis sways in the wind, occasionally tapping you in the head.

I love tall plants, and below is a tour of some of the more interesting and robust ones that work for me, keeping in mind I've got sticky clay. And we're talking herbaceous perennials, ones that grow 4, 6, 10+ feet in a single season. Without this added height, I'd have to wait a decade for shrubs and small trees, and wouldn't benefit from a long bloom time, or even any blooms at all. These tall perennials add much needed structure, a sense of privacy, safe perches for birds, and are pollinating insect magnets. Plus, I don't have to get on my hands and knees—we're on equal footing. Like Christopher Walken's character on Saturday Night Live, the man who's very afraid of plants, I like to look my garden in the eyes. But I don't glue googly eyes on to each plant. Not yet, anyway.

Eupatorium purpureum
Joe Pye Weed
(4-10')
There are lots of eupatoriums, and I have several species. It's fairly familiar, I think, but it's important because every species I have draws in the bugs like crazy. I have eupatoriums that are two feet

tall, six feet, and ten feet. The taller ones bring a delicate tropical feel to the garden with their foliage and thick, speckled trunks, like some sort of bamboo.

Coreopsis tipteris
Tall Tickseed
(7')
Last fall I put in a half dozen plugs of this coreopsis not expecting to see 7' tall whispy stands this summer. I am in love with this unique coreopsis. And it holds up very well to our high Nebraska winds while taking up so little real estate.

Filipendula rubra 'Venusta'
Queen of the Prairie
(4')
I can't stand the Barbie-pink blooms in May, even though they smell like roses (when roses used to have scent, remember those days?). I prefer the much more interesting copper after-blooms that last all summer and through fall. There are short cultivars, notably the dwarf Filipendula ulmaria 'Flora Plena', but there are also white blooming and gold-leaved cultivars that get to 4'.

Verbena hastata
Blue Vervain
(7')
I admit the blooms of this guy are boring—you can't see them unless you have a zoom lens. However, its candelabra winter form is appealing to me, and I use it to brace other tall perennials nearby, like ironweed.

Vernonia fasciculata
Prairie or Common Ironweed
(6-7')
Need to be propped up after the first summer storm, but the dark purple thunderhead-esque blooms bring in butterflies. It's named for the copper, paintbrush-like after bloom, which turns to a fluffy seed easily carried off in fall.

Vernonia alitissima 'Jonesboro Giant'
Giant Ironweed
(12' +)

I was on a six month mail order waitlist for this king of the herbaceous perennials. It was found in Arkansas, and as per the catalog description: "The giant clumps sway a bit in the breeze, but so does the Sears Tower. Warning lights may be required in some jurisdictions... please check local flight path maps." In its first season this ironweed went straight to twelve feet, so here's hoping for more next summer.

Salvia azurea 'Nekan'
Blue Pitcher Sage
(3-5')
This is a sky-blue sport found in north Lincoln (Nekan = Nebraska + Kansas), a true native for me. And like most fall-blooming perennials you can pinch it back, or more, up until about July 4th. You'll sacrifice height, but get more blooms. Every fall I've had hummingbirds visit my sage as they fly south.

Monarda fistulosa
Wild Bergamot
(4-5')
This native bee balm blooms a few weeks after the more common red, and is a much more appealing color than those gaudy pinks of the newer cultivars. It loses its leaves as you go down the stalks, like most monarda seem to do, so it's best to have something 2' tall in front of them. It stands strong fairly well, too.

Sanguisorba menziesii 'Dali Marble'
Variegated Burnet
(4-6')
The foliage is tipped in cream, and the small, red bottlebrush blooms atop wiry stems look like mini cattails. Blooms in late fall—is in fact the last flowering plant in my garden, well after the asters. Sometimes, an early winter will prevent it from blooming at all.

There are many other tall plants that grow well for me, and provide unique foliage and blooms across the season. Following is a longer list of plants, all alive, all thriving:

Thalictrum 'Black Stockings'
(6')
Brilliant mauve blooms in late spring on top of sturdy yet inconspicuous black stems.

Thalictrum 'Elin'
Meadow Rue
(4-5')
Late spring, dainty / whispy blooms.

Thalictrum glaucum
Yellow Meadow Rue
(4-5')
Late spring bloomer, nice blue leaves.

Liatris aspera
Rough Blazing Star
(3-4')
I call it the shorter cousin to L. ligulistylis. Blooms mid to late summer as well.

Chelone glabra
White Turtlehead
(6')
Another favorite, white turtle heads on sturdy stalks that grow in bunches. Blooms August to September. Bumble bees like the challenge.

Veronicastrum virginicum
Culver's Root
(4')
White-spiked blooms in mid to late summer, takes its time flowering while bees and wasps gorge.

Agastache cana 'Sinning' Sonoran Sunset
Giant Hyssop
(4')
Very giant for me in its spread and height. Draws in the hummingbird moths three at a time.

Aster puniceus 'Eric's Big Blue'
(Symphyotrichum)
(6')
Love this guy! Similar to A. tataricus below but doesn't spread as much.

Aster tataricus
Tatarian Aster
(5-6')
Blue / violet blooms in easily-divided clumps from September to frost.

Aster tataricus 'Jindai'
Dwarf Tatarian Aster
(4')
Blue / violet blooms tightly clustered together, from September to frost.

Rudbeckia maxima
Cabbage Leaf / Giant Coneflower
(6'-7')
Large blue leaves, blooms in late June / early July. Seed heads are incredible in winter.

Indian Grass
Sorghastrum nutans
(5-7')
Though it's not a flowering perennial, technically, the flowering spikes dangle small stamens and anthers of orange and yellow as they bloom, while the height provides much winter interest and good summer screening. Quick to establish, the base of the plant is wide and thick, providing solid cover for wildlife and nest building materials for spring birds.

Rudbeckia maxima – Giant Coneflower

Splendor in the Grass

The garden is about 1/3 of the backyard—the rest is grass, a space I've left to encourage the house's resale value. Most families want lawn. I recognize this, reluctantly.

In the southwest corner of the yard is a thirty foot elm tree, slowly recovering from the development graders that shredded its root system (I water and fertilize it religiously). The elm is also the last tall tree at the end of a small wooded area, so squirrels use it as a jumping off point to my bird feeders another forty feet into the yard.

I've got two feeders. One by the chain link fence, which catches the first wave of squirrels—often three at a time, sometimes five. This occupies them for about two days, until they make it further into the yard to the second feeder. Of course, I have squirrel logs, corn ear contraptions, and even peanuts to attempt diversions, but to little avail. The squirrels make a bee line to the feeders, even past the suet.

I marvel at the birds who visit me. Each year I see a greater variety. Before I moved in I had no idea we had cardinals in Nebraska—but really, why shouldn't we. Juncos, sparrows, blue jays, house finches, yellow finches, northern flickers, mourning doves, grackles, robins, various woodpeckers... all of them flinging out seeds they don't like from the feeder.

Since I mow about once a month, preferring both to avoid the heat and have a taller lawn that resembles prairie in its feeble way, things begin to make a home in the lush field. Funnel spider webs dot the lawn. Grasshoppers and frogs seek refuge. And small sunflowers, beneath the bird feeders, begin to bloom.

I mow around the sunflowers. One day I turned off the mower, got on my knees, and watched just how many bugs visited one tiny bloom only eight inches off the ground. It was astounding to see the activity one meager flower produced. And it made me despise my lawn a little more.

So I've started tossing bird seed everywhere. Sure, the squirrels and ground-feeding birds will get most of them, but some will take root. Some will lift small, weak flowers just past the delightfully unkempt grass, and like a searchlight they'll cast about over the vista and call in the world. I can't imagine a more wonderful selling feature for a family then a backyard full of flowers, devoid of grass. I can't think of a better way to raise a child.

The Lesser of Two Weevils

The sunflowers are vanishing. One by one, sometimes even a dozen a day, the bright yellow of Helianthus 'Lemon Queen,' a shrubby type of sunflower, is being deadheaded. I walk out every morning to find the heads either missing entirely or hanging limp from the stem. Surely it gets enough water. Maybe the soil here is contaminated, something buried by the bulldozer during grading. A fungus. More likely a fungus. But I don't have a clue.

In 2008 there must have been hundreds of blooms, in 2009 less than one hundred, and now, in 2010, maybe thirty. I turn to my trusted Google search engine and come up with nothing. A few weeks later, still ticked off, still at a loss even after talking to nursery owners and other gardeners, I Google again late into the night. This is not a euphemism.

I type in every search phrase possible: missing sunflowers, sunflower wilt, sunflower fungus, sunflower pinched, sunflower fallen, sunflower cut.... Cut. That's exactly what it looked like, and on the other annual sunflowers I planted from seed this spring, too. It's like someone came along with a scissors and nonchalantly / demonically cut the stem a few inches below the bloom, but with a sense of mischief left just enough stem so that the bloom was still attached, hanging on for dear life.

Black sunflower stem weevils. A little insect smaller than a kernel of corn, and apparently a problem for sunflower growers in the Plains. It takes its little snout thing and saws through the stem, no matter how thick, but only after laying eggs in the bloom; this machete-like act prevents others from using the flower. Over the winter, after the bloom has fallen to the ground, the weevil larvae snuggle in warmly, later to emerge as adults in late spring searching for sunflowers.

One morning I found one in a 'Lemon Queen' bloom, the head already cut. A few days later, another in a red sunflower bloom, half cut. I ground up both weevils with mulch, the snap and pop of their hard-shelled bodies one of the most satisfying sounds I'd heard in months.

From that point on, already now late September, I didn't

lose a bloom. But in the mulch, in dried, shriveled blooms, I know the weevils I missed are growing. And though I'm honestly not one to condone wanton murder, in general, the sunflowers—which other insects gorge upon—must clearly be saved for the greater good. I choose the lesser of two evils.

Thrashing

"Robin eggs are blue," I tell my wife. "That's all I know. These aren't blue." After calling downstairs to my wife's office, she's excited to check out our first bird nest, which I found in the honeysuckle vine. In the back corner of the garden, where the wood fence meets the chain link fence, a yellow honeysuckle is hiding a nest of four eggs.

When we get outside we're careful to sneak up to it, unless the parents are nearby. They are cream-colored, spotted brown, or the other way around. Each night at dinner we stare out to the garden, sometimes our food missing our mouths, waiting to see what might come flying into the honeysuckle.

Finally, we catch some reddish-brown birds, smaller than a robin. We've seen them in the cedars before. After dinner we both go to our respective computers in a race to discover they are brown thrashers, a common bird we'd not seen here before. Indeed, most "common" birds we don't see until years pass in the garden, which makes me wonder how many most people miss on a daily basis. I study up on the thrasher's incubation period, knowing that when we get back from a trip to Minnesota they'll be ready to hatch.

But when we return there is only one egg left in the nest, the others are on the ground, nearly intact but empty. That evening we watch a black and white cat climb the fence and begin nosing around in the honeysuckle, until I open the door and scare it off.

I read that it's unlikely the birds will now return to the nest to incubate the last egg, instead they may try to begin another if there's time before fall. There's not much anyone can do, though I feel a sense of guilt and culpability I've never known before. I put the garden there. I set the whole thing into play. Are the eggs any different now then a perennial?

A few days later the last egg is missing, the nest in shambles and strewn about the vine. Maybe the cat fell through, or maybe the thrashers came back and put up a fight. Maybe, against all recorded science and ornithology, the thrashers took the egg to a new home, then destroyed the nest in an act of defiance.

Confessions

The most perennials I planted in one day was around thirty. The most pots I took to be recycled at one time exceeded 100. The most money I spent on one trip to the nursery was nearly $1,000. The longest time I've taken to plant anything was three hours. The first time a wasp stung me was late in the third year. I once accidently stepped on a monarch caterpillar. I've sliced many a grub with the tip of my spade.

When one of my first trees failed, likely due to lack of watering and proper citing, the nursery gave me a replacement since it was within their one year guarantee. I thought I might be able to salvage the first tree, and told the men delivering the second just to leave the first since I was going to turn it into mulch. I now have two of the same tree, and feel like a $150 thief.

I often come into the house with yellow hands having smooshed hundreds of aphids on the milkweeds.

I harvest aster, liatris, coneflower, baptisia, ironweed, sunflower and other seed, then walk along the back fence tossing it over from behind the cover of a cedar tree.

I drive down the road with jars and assorted nut canisters full of seed, holding them out of the window or sunroof until they're empty. This is not a euphemism.

The first time I let my wife take a cutting, from some sanguisorba, it tore my heart. But I'm better now—and ready for the next time she asks.

I've turned into a plant snob. Which isn't hard to do when one looks at the landscapes around him. Arborvitae, geraniums, daylilies, and barberries don't make a garden, let alone a hospitable place for much wildlife.

When I was a child I squatted while playing outside, never kneeling.

Haven't made love in the garden. At least not in the way we think of such things.

Have realized it is possible to both curse from the bottom of your stomach and be transfigured in wondrous awe at the very same moment. Suppose this may be as close to understanding god as a human can get. Which makes the garden the intersection of heaven and hell, and a perfect place to make love, at least in the way we think of such things.

Salvia azurea 'Nekan' – Pitcher Sage

It's so hard to be blue in the garden, and yet each opened bell of a bloom from tall stalks reflects the summer sky. In evenings, exactly an hour before sunset, a ruby throated hummingbird makes his daily visit. He only spends a second or two, darts away, completely vanishes, then reappears at the red sunflower or white boltonia before returning to the sage. In autumn each absent bloom reveals a small pod with freckle-sized seeds. This sage is most at home here, less than ten minutes from where it was first found, a native to southern Nebraska and northern Kansas. It takes two names as one, crossing many borders—day into night, summer into fall, blooming as long as it pleases, smelling of crushed juniper.

Where I'm From

Less than a mile north is a main BNSF rail yard, the Burlington Northern and Santa Fe lines now one conglomerate who both, in the late 1800s, vied for my family's business as they and thousands of other Mennonites immigrated from Russia to the Great Plains. In cold winter nights the sound of railcars colliding together is like thunder as long trains of Wyoming coal are linked with long trains of shipping containers.

Less than a mile south is Pioneers Park, where on the far west end a few dozen bison and elk roam several acres. Perhaps their migratory instincts have been erased over the generations, or they may simply be latent and suppressed. Behind the barbwire fences that revolutionized borders, they pace around a small pond, rest beneath cottonwoods, stare at a small bit of prairie out beyond a dirt road and hear the same trains I hear at night. Those railroads carved up their world like they did the many native American tribes. Railroad companies advertised overseas about cheap land for sale near rail lines and new towns, land the companies got for free from the government. Foreign agents visited towns and villages to rally poor Europeans, set up ocean passage, and donate railcars for trunks, wagons, and stone implements. I imagine what this place was like as my ancestors passed through Lincoln on their way to Kansas.

As I lay waking in the morning I hear the short, sharp calls of a cardinal at the feeder, spaced every few seconds apart. To me they are a winter bird, a sharp holiday red against the faded green of invasive eastern red cedars they shelter in. The birds are home wherever they are, doing what they can in a landscape that changes radically every decade. The houses move out further, the trees move north as the earth warms. The fences and the highways dissect the land and separate us from it, making us no longer migrants but sheltered animals in a world we made without understanding the world of which we are. I hear the train cars colliding eastward toward bigger cities. I wonder if the bison can hear them, and if that call is now a primal fear. I wonder how far the hard echo reaches in the chilled morning of this late autumn, and how latent our instincts are to migrate again, one last time, beyond the lines we imagine hold us safely apart from one another, and into the world we've separated ourselves from.

Open Garden

I admit I'm a misanthrope. I'm a recluse. I need my solitude, tons of it, like dark chocolate. And though my back garden is my cloister, there are times I will walk through the garden gate, fling it open wildly, and tour the front beds around dusk. This is the time when people take walks. Young couples with strollers, middle-aged women walking dogs, older folks visiting kids from out of town. I hope that, as they walk by, they'll glance over, catch a peek of the garden path beyond, and stop mid stride. Maybe I'll look up from my pretend weeding and they'll holler from the street, "That's quite a backyard you got." And I'll shout back, "Thank you." We'll stand there for a few seconds, awkward, I waiting to sense that they want to see it, but it's the backyard, a garden, it's private, it's mine, and knowing they want permission and I want to give it, I'll take a few steps and say, "You want to see the garden?"

Maybe they'll have a child with them, maybe they will become children themselves. Maybe as they pass through the side garden, under the arbor and river birch, and out into the open of 300 flowering perennials, they'll ask what something is, ask to smell a bloom, lightly tease a finger across the wild senna or amsonia. Maybe they'll notice the caterpillars on the milkweed. It won't be a long visit, but the echo will reverberate in us for days.

I don't want to show off the garden, not as much as you might think. I want to share it, which surprises me. It shocks me, especially as I'm so protective of it and myself. Last spring my wife and I had a small garden party for friends in May, and one couple brought their twins, about two years old. Each had to touch the fountain, feel the sheet of water pulse over their hands and slide mysteriously into the ground. The next day I did the same.

Main Back Garden in July

Garden Spider

Draped four feet off the ground, between the clump river birch and the verbena, is a web about eighteen inches in diameter. In the middle rests a plump, female yellow garden spider. There are a few others, all nearly the same distance off the ground—one by the aster tataricus, another by the ironweed.

Her legs are like black toothpicks, and as I see a fly land in the web, their dexterity and pinpoint accuracy are a marvel as they first hold then rotate prey near the silk-spraying abdomen. I am terrified of spiders, but know she is harmless. I try to remember Charlotte's Web, and the knowledge that these are nonpoisonous, beneficial spiders. The wolf spider I found in the lawn near my sandled feet are also beneficial, but venomous. My garden is, perhaps, becoming more than I bargained for—it's hard to keep up with all that's going on, coming through.

With yet another glut of grasshoppers, perhaps holdovers from 2009, I have a great idea. I walk over to the switchgrass, sneak up on a grasshopper, and swiftly close my hand around it. It claws and tickles, then seems to bite at my palm as I rush it over, wildly tossing it into the web. It struggles, and in so doing drops an inch or two, and almost freeing itself only becomes tangled again.

The spider stops and starts, judging who knows what from the vibration of her web—the size of prey, the distance, its orientation, if it will escape or not. Soon she rushes over and within a split second has paralyzed then encased it with silk—a substance that is far stronger than steel or even Kevlar.

In case you think me cold or unkind, I encourage you to visit my 5,000 grasshoppers and diminishing perennials. I also want you to know that I capture and release all sorts of spiders, boxelder, and lady bugs from inside my house. My wife rescues frogs who've fallen into her office's egress window well.

A few times a week, as I pass the web over the early fall, I try to toss the spider a free meal. Sometimes I can't capture a grasshopper, sometimes they wiggle free of the web. And when, one autumn day, I see the web torn and abandoned, I read up on the spider's lifecycle, how the females die before winter. I feel a gentle loss and sadness that surprises me, as if a friend has moved away. Each day the web rips a bit more as the leaves turn color. I know that something new was spelled out for me here, this year in my garden, but I don't yet know how to interpret it.

Aster laevis 'Bluebird' – Smooth Aster

In September where there should be a bloom, there's a shadow darting, hovering, pulsating like some tiny heart. Pollen springs into the air, and when the shadow moves a yellow center settles into its dusky violet petals. Yet the shadow is only part of a larger cloud, a finger, a kaleidoscope of action settling and rising, settling and rising. Every bee in the county must be hear, every fly, every moth, every butterfly, every wasp. Before the chicken wire there was the rabbit, who in spring ate two stalks, so the full potential isn't realized. From dawn to dusk the shrubby perennial hums, almost lifts off the ground itself. Stop to listen, place your ear close, and you might hear the ocean—a thousand messages crashing against the shore of hunger.

The Last Cosmo

Late October, nearly November, and the frosts have come. Only a few asters, a burnet, and some hidden annuals have made it through, shaded my trees or shrubs, or in the open saved by a light breeze. Near the back of the garden, in a dark space, I tossed seeds from packets of annuals I received free in the mail. There were some chocolate sunflowers, gaudy orange cosmos I knew the insects would like, and pink cosmos from years ago, a packet I found buried in a closet. I didn't know if any would grow.

It took them a while to get started, and they never made it past two feet, the three or so stalks I saw. Too little sunlight, I figured, beside a tall red cedar. But this space stayed warm into autumn, and looking out from the dining room window the garden was already brown—except for that beacon of soft pink, a Pepto Bismal speck in the corner. I rushed out with my jacket on, and the unfurled cosmo—with swiss cheese holes torn in its petals—had a bumble bee at its center. Below the bloom was another beginning to open, but neither would make it through the night.

The next day, after much deliberation, fighting my instincts and loathsome attitude toward most annuals, I headed out with pot and spade and dug up the cosmo. I put in the back of the garage hoping it might survive winter, that we both might. In spring I'll bring it back out, harden it off, and dig it into the same place—both of us grounded in the familiarity of that soil.

Twilight Geese in Autumn

A few evenings ago I made my nightly pilgrimage around the garden and yard. After inspecting and filling the dozens of holes dug by migrating robins and brown thrashers, I made my way to check on the fall foliage of the birches, maple, and willow.

Along the back fence is an opening that looks out to my neighbor's three acres, and in the distance—about 200 feet—is a thick stand of mature trees on the edge of their property. Where that stand of trees ends and meets the thin line that runs along the back of my lot, is a small pond which marks the end of a long flyway, if you will, reaching back across many acreages running parallel to my neighborhood.

An autumn dusk is always breathtaking. The air is crisper and drier, the sunlight sharper, the musk of rich decay feeding new soil sweet and thick and reminiscent of the woods I would explore growing up in Minnesota. I am always home when I smell this air, holding it as close and far inside me as possible with each deep breath.

My chilling body leans against the chain link fence, and I can hear in some great distance Canadian geese—another call home for me. The cries shout far in this air, at this time, and I know they are searching out their nightly place among the cornfields not too far away, or the many small ponds that dot a nearby park. I don't think they are coming closer, but moving south, away from me, as they do this time of year.

But their calls remain constant, neither growing fainter nor louder. It's like my heartbeat, racing north, leaning slightly into the wind and suddenly darting right or left to catch an impulse, a desire.

I can't see them. Behind the cedars and elms is where they must be, but I am so low here, between the trees, a small gap in the line, I'll never see them.

Suddenly one lone call pierces loudly, rushes forward like a warning, a groping in the dark. I hear their wings like someone slipping on a warm coat in winter. Then there they are, no more than 20-30 feet off the ground, mapping the earth in front of me. A perfect "V" of two dozen birds, pushing and pulling air, stable in the dichotomy of their actions, pulsing from east to west. I've never been so close.

The edge of the "V" closest to me is missing a bird, and as the formation slides by so low that for a moment I childishly think I can reach up, hook on and be carried away, I believe they have made a place for me.

And they have. The moment lasts all but two or three seconds, but I no longer exist in the same way that I did before. I am no longer the same person. As the calls slide over the horizon chasing the last faint yellow and magenta sunlight, I am here and nowhere, far away and closer to my home.

Stay still. Don't breathe. Be ready. They may come around again.

Garden Entrance in 2011

Native Plant & Prairie Ecosystem Resources

Purchase Plants

Prairie Nursery
http://www.prairienursery.com
Prairie Moon Nursery
http://www.prairiemoon.com
Nebraska Statewide Arboretum
http://arboretum.unl.edu

Native Plant Information

Ladybird Johnson Wildflower Center
http://www.wildflower.org
Pollinator Partnership
http://www.pollinator.org
The Xerces Society
http://xerces.org
*Bringing Nature Home: How Native Plants Sustain
Wildlife in Our Gardens (Timber Press)*
– Douglas Tallamy

Native Plant / Wildlife Blogs

Native Plants & Wildlife Gardens
http://nativeplantwildlifegarden.com
The Prairie Ecologist
http://prairieecologist.com

Get Involved

Monarch Watch / Monarch Waystation Certification
http://www.monarchwatch.org
National Wildlife Federation / Backyard Wildlife
Habitat Certification
http://www.nwf.org
Lawn Reform Coalition
http://www.lawnreform.org

Benjamin Vogt is the author of the poetry collection *Afterimage* (SFA Press), as well as two chapbooks. He has a Ph.D. from the University of Nebraska-Lincoln and an M.F.A. from The Ohio State University. Benjamin's nonfiction and poetry have been nominated for a Pushcart Prize, and have appeared in over fifty journals, newspapers, anthologies, and textbooks, including *American Life in Poetry, Crab Orchard Review, Diagram, Hayden's Ferry Review, ISLE, Orion, Puerto del Sol, Sou'wester, Subtropics, The Sun,* and *Verse Daily.* He lives in Lincoln, Nebraska with his wife, where they dream of restoring an acreage to prairie, opening a boutique nursery, and hosting an artist residency program. He owns Monarch Gardens, prairie garden consulting and design, and writes a weekly column for Houzz.com.

Other Books & Manuscripts by Benjamin Vogt

Morning Glory: A Story of Family & Culture in the Garden

When a son reflects on a childhood of gardening with his mother, he finds clues to a family lineage built around silences, distance, and forgetfulness. Eventually, his mother begins to openly reveal a past that confronts the author's own dark nature. In the history of gardens there are great tragedies and triumphs, and in the garden we continue to discover our truest selves.

Memoir
247mp. / 75,000 words
(unpublished)

Afterimage: Poems

From Oklahoma to Minnesota, Ohio to Nebraska, Benjamin Vogt traces his life through his ancestors who settled the Great Plains in the 1800s. With poems based on black & white family photographs, and in a rich array of forms, *Afterimage* reaches through prairie history until grass becomes skin, and light becomes shadow.

SFA Press, 2012

Turkey Red: A Memoir

A lost son of Oklahoma traces his Mennonite roots through the echo of his grandmother. The culture and history of Plains Indians, German settlers, and prairie wildlife lead the author into America's frontier legacy—a wound left unhealed until family is discovered again through the vanishing landscapes around us.

250mp / 80,000 words